Family Secrets and Lies

Family Secrets and Lies

Helen Woods

Library of Congress Control Number: 2011901182
ISBN: Hardcover   978-1-4568-5826-1
                 Softcover   978-1-4568-5825-4
                 Ebook   978-1-4568-5827-8

To order additional copies of this book, contact:
Xlibris Corporation
0-800-644-6988
www.xlibrispublishing.co.uk
Orders@xlibrispublishing.co.uk
301251

I dedicate this book to Sue, Stephen, and Wayne—
three very important people in my life.

Chapter One

The darkness of the night was broken only by the ethereal light that crept in through the glass window above the bedroom door. The silence was broken by the quiet crying of the frail little girl in the bed who was praying for the morning to free her from the chains of darkness. She was totally unaware of the rain tap-dancing on the window. She was totally unaware of anything other than the pain that tortured her.

Tightly curled up like a baby in the safety of the womb, she could not find any feelings of peace, safety, or security. Joanna tried to hide herself under the big, colourful, fluffy eiderdown that her nanna had made her, but her one precious possession let her down.

The night was finally almost over. At last Joanna could see the sun rising, through the rosy glow it cast through the gap in the curtains. It was a dark, depressing room, although Joanna was unaware of this as lots of rooms were like that. A lot of people had utility furniture in the post-war years; her wardrobe and dressing table were made of this. And with the brown linoleum on the floor, it was dark, although her mum had tried to brighten it with the white distemper on the walls. Nanna's eiderdown was very pretty with bright colours, which she had quilted from Mum and her two aunties' old dance dresses. Joanna would lie and look at the different patterns and try to imagine what it would be like to wear the original dresses, dancing the night away, laughing and very happy.

Once again her tears beat her control, and she hid under the bedclothes to try and hide them. She must not do anything to wake one of the little ones and make her mother angry; she was only too aware of what her mother may do if she was in a temper. Eventually, she fell into a nightmare-filled sleep. They were a compilation of the terrible events that littered her twelve years of life. The happy times tried to break through, but it was as if her subconscious knew she could not allow anything but evil memories.

The happiest time in her life, apart from when she was at her nanna's, was the eighteen months she had spent in hospital with poliomyelitis. A two-year-old child has no comprehension of time, but although she couldn't walk and needed help to do most things, which again is almost normal for a two-year-old, Joanna was very happy. The nurses were very kind and would spend time with her, trying to help her pass the time, very difficult for a small child who could not walk.

Although her memories were distorted, she did remember coming home from hospital, mainly because her mother and nanna did a lot of shouting.

Mummy cried and shouted, 'How on earth am I supposed to cope? They say she may never walk! Or at least not without a great deal of physiotherapy and help. How can I cope with a kid in a wheelchair?' Her tears were due to anger and not sadness. 'I have Peter running around my heels, and another one is due any day now. I cannot cope.'

'Will you stop snivelling and feeling sorry for yourself,' Nanna cried out. 'You should take more care if you can't cope with the number of kids you seem intent on having, and I will guarantee you, you will not be the one caring for our Joanna. I will see to that! You are incapable of caring for a child who needs any more than feeding and keeping clean.'

Nanna was a fair, petite lady who had strength her size denied.

'You should remember she is the one who is ill! She is the one who needs love, care, and attention, not you! You go home and leave her here with me and Val. I will make you a promise—she will walk again no matter what the doctors say.'

A happy little smile crossed the face of the sleeping child as the memories of the years she lived with her nanna and granddad came in her dreams.

They lived in a pebble-dashed prefab, one of the houses that had been put up at the end of the war until the councils had the time and equipment needed to replace the houses lost to the German bombs. They had a kitchen that was fitted with a cooker and fridge, amazing for the post-war time, two bedrooms, and a lounge with a modern hearth and fire. And in the hall, a toilet and bathroom, that even had a big heated towel rail over the bath; this heated the bathroom as well as warmed the towels. The houses in the area that had survived the war had no fridge, bathroom, or indoor toilet.

Joanna was lying awake, remembering the happy times sitting around a blazing coal fire that cast dancing patterns on the walls, dressed in warm flannelette pyjamas [that her nanna made from old sheets] which had been warmed for her while she was in the bath, drinking her mug of Horlicks that only Nanna could make right; she had a funny little jug and a metal thing that she moved quickly up and down to make it frothy. Granddad would toast bread in front of the fire and spread it with butter. Truly delicious!

The wireless would be playing, and Nanna would be rocking in her chair—knitting, crocheting, or sewing—making clothes for her or even a cuddly toy for her to play with.

One of them would then carry her to bed, and she would lie in the big feather mattress, which felt like a field of candy floss. Then one would read her a story, while the other massaged and exercised her thin little legs; she understood this was to keep them strong until she could walk again.

At Christmas time, Joanna and her friends used to sit around the radio as Father Christmas would come and ask them what they would like for Christmas if they were good girls and boys. Each child's face would light up with the magic of it all and talk about it constantly, sometimes driving their parents crazy.

None of the children realised Jo's granddad had a microphone at the other side of the wall, and he had drilled a hole to connect it to the radio. He would sit in the bedroom next to the sitting room and talk to the children.

Jo fondly remembered the year three of her friends—Jennifer, Josephine, and Angela—asked for a doll's pram, and she said she would love one as well. Her grandparents realised this was not practical from a wheelchair, and they couldn't afford one, so Granddad made a pram body out of wood and beautifully carved carnations in the side of it; he stained and polished it to a beautiful shine, and her nanna used an old navy gabardine coat to make the hood and apron as well as pretty blankets. They then mounted it on a rocker so Joanna could play and it wouldn't run away from her. The only thing she was aware of was the amount of time they spent in their shed, and she had been told to keep out.

This was her prized possession for many years until it vanished after she had left home, along with a book Uncle Syd had bought for her fifth birthday. All of the adults there said he was crackers buying David Copperfield for a bairn's fifth birthday, but she was thrilled. Uncle Syd told them not to worry and that Joanna would read it. And she did. Nanna had taught her to read to keep her occupied.

When she was eight years old, this changed. Daddy was going away, but this had not affected her as, due to him being in the navy, he was not there much anyway.

However, her mother had insisted she go back to live with her, her reason being that Daddy had gone to live in Wales. And he had said, because she didn't live at home, he was going to ask the courts to let her live with him.

Joanna had innocently asked why Mummy hadn't gone with him.

'Just because he can earn more money, and a house came with the job, it is no reason for me to move. And I like living in Hull.'

She calmed herself down and then explained that she had found a new daddy for them all. By this time, Joanna had three brothers and a sister, and they were moving into a bigger house with four bedrooms. Now Joanna could have a room of her own. This meant nothing as she had her own room at Nanna's. Although there were a lot of tears shed at leaving Nanna's, she would always be able to go for weekends and holidays, and the excitement of moving to a new house on a new estate, and add to this a promise of her own room instead of sharing as she had when she had gone home for weekends, made up for the disappointment.

Nanna had been there all day helping with the move. Once everyone was fed and the children bathed, they were put to bed at six thirty. They were all tired, and the little ones fell into deep sleep but not Joanna. She was aware of shouting from downstairs.

Her little bed was very comfortable and looked very pretty with the eiderdown Nanna had made her. Joanna had been content lying there, watching the light fade through the pretty curtains also made by Nanna. The sun made the carnations on them dance. They would be her favourite flowers forever.

Raised voices brought her back to reality, Nanna's voice rising above her mother's. She sounded very angry. It frightened her, and she started weeping.

Grown-ups arguing always had this effect, maybe because these two arguing seemed to always involve her, or the babies Mummy kept having.

Her fear was real, but she had to know what was happening. Her calipers were removed when she was in bed, so she lowered herself to the floor, thankful she had a thick patterned carpet on the floor that helped quieten the sound of her dragging herself to the door.

'I know you have brought her home only to help you look after this one. Sam says it isn't his. Is that why he has left you?'

Nanna was almost screaming.

Mummy shouted back.

'It has nothing to do with you. It is my life! She is my daughter you know, not yours! And it is up to me where she lives. You have always favoured her, even over our Jean and Eric's two and our Madge and Bill's three. Anyway she is staying here, and there is nothing you can do about it! So I will thank you if you will keep your nose out and mind your own business.'

Nanna sounded even more angry as she replied. 'Do not give me that load of rubbish. Our Jean and Madge understand why she has needed me, and their kids know I love them all. You would not have wanted her back if she couldn't walk, and it's down to me and your father that she can, albeit with her calipers on! And you had better keep up the exercises if you know what is good for you. I have promised her a pair of normal shoes for her eleventh birthday, and your father and I do not break our promises.'

Nanna went quiet, but Joanna heard her come into the hall to get her coat off the hook.

'As for my other grandbairns, the five of them know how much I love them all, but they have more brains and common sense than you. They love our Jo and understand she needs more care than they do, and like me, they thank God they have not gone through what she has. If you had half the brain they have, your daughter may have been with you all these years. I am going now, but just think on what I have told you, and it will not just be me you upset but your father as well.'

The back door banged shut, and she could hear Nanna wheeling her bike through the passage. She dragged herself back to bed as quick as she could, just getting under the eiderdown as her mother burst into the room.

'Right, you spoilt young lady, this is where things change. You are with me now, and this is where you will stay. No more pampering. You will earn your keep, and do your share of the jobs around here.'

Her voice was not raised but quietly menacing and scarier than shouting.

'In the morning, you will be up and dressed by seven. You will see to Peter and Harold and get them off to school, before the bus comes for you. Just think of the shame you have brought me, and remember you owe me for looking after you. A bus coming for a handicapped kid in my house! Showing the world the cross I have to bear. I might as well shout it from the rooftops. What will the neighbours think? Only thick kids go on them buses,' she spat the words at her.

'Your precious Nanna needn't worry. I will do your exercises. I want you at the normal school. That will mean the neighbours will stop talking, and you can do more around here, like bringing the lads home from school for a start!' She turned and walked out of the room without so much as a glance, not caring what effect her words had on her daughter. She switched the light off and, slamming the door, left the room. Joanna had been too afraid to say she was frightened of the dark and had lain awake for hours, frightened by the strange shapes the dark conjured up.

Chapter Two

Back in the present, Joanna tried hard to go back to sleep. But this was impossible due to the pain in her back and even more so by the pain in her mind. In the early morning light, she lay there, trying to work out how to escape, although knowing this was impossible. During the time back at her mother's, the miserable life she was forced to live had almost masked her happy memories of living with her nanna.

The first year had passed very quickly, as it does when you are very busy, and not many good things are happening.

Her life had settled into a hard routine. Out of necessity, she had learned how to put on her boots and calipers in almost lightning speed, and how to look after her brothers, with Mum looking after Lynne, the new baby.

At seven years old, Peter had been very good at learning how to help Joanna. Even though he was so young, he had been doing some of the tasks before she came home. He adored his sister and positively preened when people said they looked alike.

This was very true. They could have been mistaken for twins, each having an abundance of rich auburn hair. Peter's was kept short to try to control his unruly curls, whereas Joanna's fell in a glorious cascading waterfall of curls, almost reaching her waist.

Due to the admiration this brought from everyone, her mother had let it grow as it distracted the attention away from the calipers.

They both had big brown eyes, which shone and reflected the light so much that they sparkled. As Peter was tall for his age and Joanna was small for hers, they looked like twins.

Harold was completely different. Overweight, blond, and blue eyed, he had no features similar to the older two, and as he was the apple of his mother's eye, he had been spoilt, which had resulted in him being very immature and slow to learn. Malcolm and Lynn were also blond and blue eyed; no one thought anything about this as Mum was a blue-eyed blonde.

The day they moved house, a friend of Mother's had come to live with them. They had known Jim Wilkinson most of their lives. His family lived opposite Nanna's, and he had two sisters and a brother were around Joanna's age. In the beginning, he had been really good to live with. He would play games with them. He loved gardening and would let them help him. Joanna especially liked it when the tomatoes were ripe enough to pick as she would eat them in the greenhouse. Jim would laugh and tell her they were good for her. The smell of tomato plants in the green house would always be a favourite for her.

Her mother would get angry at the time he spent with the children, especially the oldest two. Even as a child, Joanna knew this was jealousy but could not understand why it was different with the younger children. Her mother had told her she couldn't do her exercises anymore but that Jim would do them.

'Your nanna will only nag me if someone doesn't waste their time on them,' she would say repeatedly.

Joanna knew this was because Mum was putting on a lot of weight, and from previous times, she also knew this meant Mum was pregnant again.

What was strange was that this baby was never talked about; it was as if she wasn't expecting. But Joanna knew she was because Nanna was crocheting baby clothes again. And she would sit with her and make bootees. She had been taught very young how to do all forms of needlework, as she couldn't run around playing games.

It must have been about six months after they had moved in that her mum started to look really ill, and Jo thought she had stopped caring about herself. Mum's beautiful shiny blonde hair that was always styled into a pageboy and had a beam of light that moved though it whenever Mummy moved her head, looked dull, lank, and hung in a lifeless straggly mess. It looked dirty like it needed washing. She had gained a lot of weight and had stopped getting dressed unless she was going out. She spent her time sitting around the sitting room in one of the leather-look brown chairs next to the coal fire, wearing a tatty old candlewick dressing gown.

Make up was a thing of the past, and she looked so pale and ill without it.

One night Jim came into her bedroom explaining that Mummy wasn't well, that Nanna was on her way, and that she would sleep in the boys' room where he had also put Lynne's cot. He was obviously distressed and worried. His hair reminded her of a wacky professor out of the Billy Bunter stories. He wouldn't answer her questions and just carried her into the boy's bedroom.

Throughout the night, there was lots of comings and goings outside the room. The three younger ones slept through, but Joanna and Peter lay awake, too frightened to sleep. Either Nanna or Jim kept coming in to tell them everything would be all right. They had worked out that this could be because of the new baby.

Dawn was breaking through the windows highlighting how crowded this bedroom was with a double and single bed as well as a cot. It was a good job. It had built-in wardrobes as there was no room for the utility furniture Joanna and her mummy had. Joanna was thinking about space and realised that with only three bedrooms, she would soon have to share her room with Lynne.

Nanna came in with two steaming mugs of Horlicks and a plate of digestive biscuits.

'Sit up you two, quietly, so you don't wake the others, and be careful not to spill.' She passed them their drinks and put the plate on the bed between them both. 'You have been good all night, so get the drinks and try to get a bit of sleep. Mummy is doing very well, and your new baby will be here very soon. And everyone will be fine then.' She left the room smiling at them.

'I wonder what it will be. Shall we think of some names? You never know Mummy might let us choose what name it is given.' Joanna was very excited she had never been there when one of the babies had arrived. She was secretly hoping for another sister. Three brothers were enough for anyone.

True to her word, when the sun was up and shining, casting shadows on the walls, and making the dust in the air look as though it was dancing like fairy diamonds, Nanna came back into the room, carrying a little baby that was the most beautiful thing they had ever seen.

'This is your baby sister. Isn't she beautiful? Look at those big blue eyes. Even without any hair she is gorgeous, and that will grow soon enough.'

Nanna held her so they could look at her. She wasn't completely bald. Her head was covered in what looked like dainty spider webs creating what looked like a halo of white fluff surrounding the cutest little face. She was all wrinkled but was still so pretty. Joanna was speechless, and Peter sat with his mouth open, just staring at her.

After they had oohed and aahed for a few minutes, Nanna wrapped the baby in her blanket and said, 'Right, you two just lie quiet until the others wake up. I expect sleep will be pointless now for either of you, but lie quietly. You never know you may get another surprise.' She was smiling as she left the room.

Peter whispered, 'Jo, why did she say that, and she had such a funny look on her face?'

'I don't know. Maybe it is because she has been up all night and is tired.'

'Well, I think she looked like grown-ups do on Christmas Eve, and that is not for ages yet.'

He did not like secrets, and you could see it in his face.

They snuggled down in Peter's bed and were drifting off when the door opened again, and Jim came in carrying their baby sister.

'Oh, Jim, have you brought her back to see us again.' Joanna sat up excitedly.

As Pete sat up, he said, 'Nanna has already shown us her, but we don't mind seeing her again. She is so cute.'

They looked at the little bundle Jim was uncovering.

'Pete, look at her. This is magic. Her hair was white. Now it is brown. How can that happen?' Jo exclaimed. Jim was laughing at their faces, and this woke Harold.

'What's up? What's going on? Will you all shut up? I want to sleep!' he grumbled without even turning to look at them.

'Now, son, don't be so grumpy. Come and see what I have here,' Jim tried to cajole him.

'Don't want to,' Harold mumbled.

Jo had shuffled closer to get a better look.

'Jim, how has her hair changed colour?' Jo was still trying to work it out as the door opened and Nanna came in carrying another little bundle with white hair.

'Pete, Harold, look. Nanna has another one. They're twins.' Jo looked at her nanna, and bursting with excitement, asked, 'What are they, Nanna? Two girls or is there a boy

Nanna was laughing at the faces of the older two. Harold still hadn't moved, and Malcolm was still asleep.

'Two girls,' she said. 'You have twin sisters. Isn't that good? They are both fit and well. Your mummy has done so well but is very tired now and needs some sleep.'

'So do I,' Harold grumbled.

'Oh, shut up, misery,' cried Peter. 'Look at these babies, two of them.'

'Leave me alone. I have enough brothers and sisters. Don't want any more.'

He climbed out of bed and stormed out of the room, slamming the door behind him. They heard him go into his mother's room.

'Mum, wake up. They won't let me sleep. Tell them all to shut up, and I don't want any more kids in the place,' he moaned.

Jim placed his baby on the bed and left the room. He was obviously angry when he shouted, 'Come out of there, you spoilt little brat. Get back in your own room or go downstairs. Your mother does not need you snivelling round her. Get out of here now.'

Harold was obviously shocked as Jim never shouted at them; he left their room and went into the bathroom. Jim came back and picked up the baby telling Nanna they should be put in the cot that was in Jo's room

'I cannot believe it. Val is crying because Harold is upset. She said I should have let him get in bed with her,' he was telling Nanna quietly

'You shouldn't be surprised. She has always spoilt him, but she will find that will have to change now. Lynne is not two yet, and she has two more to look after. I'm sorry, Jim, but you will have to do something so there are no more.'

The children didn't hear his answer. And very soon they were up and dressed. Peter had helped Jo with her boots and calipers

Chapter Three

Jo froze in fear. What was that noise? Something had penetrated her thoughts. She strained to listen. Who was it? It could be one of the little ones.

The familiar creak her mother's bedroom door gave was unmistakable. Her mind was reeling. It can't be Jim. He never comes twice in one night. Then she heard the back bedroom door open and realised it was her mother that was up. One of the boys must be awake. She knew she should get up and see what was wrong. If it was her mother, she would only smack them and tell them to go back to sleep, making them cry all the more. As she tried to get out of bed, the pain in her back stopped her. It felt as if her pyjama jacket was stuck to her back. She turned and looked in the dressing table mirror and was shocked to see the blood that had soaked through and was now drying out, stuck to her.

She ventured carefully onto the landing just as her mother was coming out of the boys' room.

'What are you doing up? It's only six o'clock.' She was looking very angry.

Jo quickly turned around so her mother could see her back.

'Please help me. I can't get my jacket off, please help me,' she begged.

Val was obviously shocked. *Oh my god, I have gone too far this time,* she thought to herself. 'Come into the bathroom. You will have to lay in the bath to get it off.' She turned the taps on and put the plug in.

'You might learn now that you have done wrong and never do it again, won't you? It's about time you learnt you can't look like you do and expect men to leave you alone, so maybe you will learn to leave my man alone and find your own, although twelve is a bit young to start.' It was as if she was really talking to herself.

Joanna was pleasantly surprised how gently her mum helped her into the bath and used the warm water to soak the pyjama jacket off her

'I am sorry, Jo. I should not have gone this far. I just saw red when I saw you on your knees doing that to Jim. I have gone too far.'

Joanna kept quiet and enjoyed the gentleness that was given by her mum.

Very carefully Val helped her out of the bath, patted her dry, applied ointment and dressings to the weals Jim's belt had created on her back. Then after putting on clean pyjamas, she helped Jo back into bed.

'Now you try to rest. I will stay up and see to the boys. You will have to have a few days off school. I will bring you some breakfast when the boys have gone to school.'

After the soothing warm bath and the dressing easing her discomfort, Jo quickly drifted off into a soothing sleep.

They now lived in a four-bedroom house, having got a transfer from the council after the twins were born, so the boys had a room; Lynne, Barbara, and Patricia [the twins] had a room; and Jo had the box room to herself so she slept through the morning noises of everyone rising.

When she woke up late morning, her mother told her to stay in bed, and if her nanna was to come around, she must tell her she wasn't well, and most importantly, she was to not let her nanna or anyone else see her back.

The bruises took about three weeks to heal; the cuts healed a little quicker but looked as if there would be some scarring.

Jim had not come near her during this time. Maybe he had learned his lesson, and maybe the nightmare would stop now.

The twins were now three years old, and as Nanna had said about hair and eye colouring changing, they both had blue eyes and blonde hair, and were like two peas in a pod. Mummy kept a red ribbon round Barbara's wrist so she knew who was who.

There was another addition, John, who was four months old and was the double of Harold.

Mummy spent most of her time playing with the three younger boys and left the girls to Jim and Joanna. Peter realised Mum preferred boys to girls but couldn't figure out where he fit, and why Mummy didn't love him.

They would find out later in their lives that Joanna and Peter were the only two belonging to their daddy. The rest were Jim's who Mummy had been seeing for a long time

The older two were inseparable, and their father had pushed until Mummy agreed to let them go on holiday with him.

Chapter Four

They had a fabulous holiday. It was good to spend some quality time together, and especially after the nerves all three felt for the first day or two.

Dad lived in a small apartment, so he had hired a cottage in Beau Maris that is about seven miles north-east of Bangor. The cottage had views over the Menai Straits and the far off mountains of Snowdonia. They spent many happy hours walking through the narrow streets of Beau Maris and looking round the famous castle, which was built by Edward 1 in 1295. He chose the site because Beau Maris is Norman French for 'beautiful marsh', and this was the last castle to be built in Wales.

The seafront drew them in. They would go on boat trips up and back down the straits. Pete was enthralled with the colourful sailing craft. They visited some of the very old churches in the area, the most intriguing being the parish church of St Mary and St Nicholas. This was built for the Garrison's use. There was lots to see because it was a major yachting centre, and they were there in the first two weeks of August, which was the annual yachting fortnight." in the early part of the fourteenth century. It has been much added to since then. Joanna was fascinated to know there was a Princess Joanna who was the daughter of Prince John. She died in 1237, and her coffin was even used as a 'horse trough' before the church rescued it.

There were some very good places to eat, and it was nice to be treated like adults in restaurants, but they also had a lot of fun cooking together in the cottage with their dad.

They even had a ride on the steam train that runs up the scenic railway almost to the top of Snowdonia, and the views from up there were breathtaking

All in all, they had a wonderful two weeks.

Joanna had heard Dad and Pete talking so quietly no one could overhear them, but it wasn't until their last night there that Pete took her into his confidence.

'Jo, I have been thinking, and I know this will upset you, but I am going to ask Mum if I can come and live with Dad.'

'Oh, Pete, I don't blame you. I couldn't leave Nanna and Granddad, or I would come as well. I will miss you so much, but it will be better for you. When are you going to ask her?'

'When she meets us at the railway station. Dad is coming with us so he can help if she loses it.'

Jo hugged her dad

'One day maybe I will come as well. What about Harry, Malc, and Lynne? What if they decide they want to come as well?'

Dad had a strange look on his face when he said, 'Don't worry. They won't.'

Pete had always been confused about his mother's feelings for him. However, things had been better when Jo had come home as they had a very close bond.

He had surprised himself when he realised where he wanted to live.

When they met their mother at the station, they managed to persuade her to go for a coffee in the station snack bar; it was far too noisy to talk at the station, with the noise of the steam trains and the announcements as well as the number of people travelling.

Once they were seated, just the three of them, Sam stayed out of sight.

Mum asked, 'Have you had a good time then? I hope so, seeing I have had to do all your jobs.'

Jo remained silent, while her brother said, 'Yes, it was good. We really enjoyed it, but there is something I want to ask you.' He had decided to jump straight in. 'I would like to live with my dad. Will you let me?'

Mum's face displayed total shock, and for a moment, she was speechless. 'Bloody hell! I did not expect that. Does this include you, Joanna? Because if it does, the answer is no.'

Joanna answered, 'No, Mum, I will not leave you and my nanna.'

'Good, because I cannot manage with you both gone, but if you are so ungrateful for what I have done for you, and Joanna will do your share of the work, then clear off with him. You deserve each other, but you take nothing with you other than what is in your case. I presume your father is hiding somewhere here, afraid to meet me.'

'I am not hiding, Val. I am right here.' Sam was behind her. 'Will you two leave us alone for a minute? You can leave your cases here.'

'Sure thing, Dad,' answered Pete as he and Joanna left the table.

They watched the animated conversation going on between their parents. It was obvious they were arguing and getting loud enough that people at the tables around them were trying hard to look as if they weren't listening. One of the staff was cleaning the laminated tables, trying to hear more. Bravely, they set off walking nearer hoping they may be able to break it up and stop the embarrassment. As they got closer, they heard Mum say 'You will never get Joanna, and yes, you are right, Harry, Malcolm, and Lynne are not yours. They are Jim's.'

This stopped the two children in their tracks. They had just heard that their brothers and sister did not have the same father, and this really shocked them both.

'I don't believe it,' whispered Pete. 'It was obvious the twins and John are Jim's, but the others. Now I know why she treats me differently.' But he really thought Mam was trying to hurt Dad by lying.

'Yes, you are right. That is why she doesn't seem to like us.'

'Maybe you should think about coming with us, Jo.'

'I can't. I am sorry, but I have to stay near Nanna and Granddad.'

Their parents turned and saw them. Dad looked shocked and sorry, realising they had heard the last part of the argument.

'Well, now you know the truth. It's better that way. Me and Jim have told the three of them, and they are calling him Daddy now, so you would have found out when we got home. Get your case, Joanna. We are leaving.'

Val got up and, without a backward glance at Sam or Peter, started walking away. Jo ran and gave her dad and brother a kiss and a hug.

'Write to me at Nanna's. Keep in touch, please.' She let go of Pete and hurried the best she could after her mother. Both children were crying but knew they had done the right thing.

Chapter Five

Joanna's exercises had continued from her coming to live with her mother. In fact that was how the nightmare with Jim had started. True to her word, Nanna had bought her a pair of proper shoes for her eleventh birthday.

She also passed her eleven plus exams and gained a place in Malet Lambert Grammar school. This had made Nanna even more proud of her. Mum complained about the cost of the uniform but had to stop when her dad sent her the money to pay for it, and bought her a BSA star rider bicycle for doing so well. It was Jo's pride and joy, in a beautiful shade of blue with gold stars climbing up the frame.

Mother had treated her a little better because she was the only child on their estate to pass the eleven plus, and the Hull Daily Mail had published this news, which gave her mother something to brag about.

Jim's visits had not stopped, even though he knew what her mother would do to her. She still carried the scars from the last time. She had to be careful Nanna never saw them.

The beating had actually helped Jim. He would remind her what her mum would do, but she was frightened more by him saying she would be taken away by social services and would never see her grandparents again. This was why she couldn't tell anyone.

She would pray he would stop drinking; sober, he could have been a really good stepdad, but his drinking was getting more frequent. Mum worked four nights a week in a local pub called the Goat and Compass, and Jo babysat while Jim went to see her mum, so four nights a week she couldn't rest.

She heard from Pete regularly. He sent letters to her at Nanna's so Mum couldn't intercept them. He was happy there although still sorry he couldn't see her. She was not allowed to go on holiday anymore. Dad wanted to go to court for custody, but Jo said no as she still wanted to be near her grandparents.

Joanna did not make many friends at school, for several reasons. She was afraid they would find out what she did with Jim. She couldn't go out with any friends or have them home, so she tried not to get too close to anyone.

The teaching staff were concerned about this because she was a very pleasant girl and an excellent pupil who had settled in very well at the high school. It was obvious she was a lonely girl, and this worried them.

The school had sent several letters home asking her mother to come in and talk to them. She ignored them all and did not attend parents' evening, her excuse being, with seven kids she did not have the time.

This left the staff worried about how they could help; it needed her mother's help as well as theirs to benefit Joanna.

Mr Smith, the English teacher, had expressed his concerns repeatedly. Joanna's work was excellent. She was definitely the star pupil for English, but sometimes the things she wrote in her essays worried him, especially if he asked her to write about home life and family.

He had been doing this more often, especially asking her to write about her family. He then asked other staff to read her work. They all agreed there was a problem, the general opinion being it was the result of being the oldest of eight, the work this involved, and missing her brother, who she was close to. And the mixture of these things could be why she displayed these problems.

If only Mr Smith had followed his hunch!

Chapter Six

When Jo was fourteen, she arrived home from school to find a neighbour looking after the kids.

'Where's my mum? Why are you looking after the little ones? Where are the twins and our John?' She knew something was wrong.

'Hold on a minute. Keep your hair on. First things first, your mum is at the infirmary with your nanna. Your granddad has had a funny turn, but he is all right, so don't worry. The three youngest are at your nanna Mary's [Jim's Mum].

'I could not manage all of them. Thank God I only have two kids. I have always said your mum deserves a bloody great medal.' Lilly was putting her coat on as she talked. 'Sorry to run, but our James and Ann will be hungry. Shout if you need any help.' As the door closed behind her, Jo collapsed in the chair, trying to think what she could do.

Lilly had said Jim [she said your dad because she didn't know any different, and Mum insisted their private life was nothing to do with anybody else] would ring as soon as he had any news.

Mum had had a phone put in; Jo knew this was also something to brag about.

Jo was smiling to herself at Lilly saying Mum worked hard looking after them all. She could not remember what Mum had ever done for her, apart from hurting her.

She even called herself Mrs Wilkinson, letting people think she and Jim were married; all of Jim's kids had his name, so Jo had to be careful not to let anyone know her name was Downie.

An hour later, Nanna Mary brought the little ones home and helped Jo bath them and get them off to bed; the others knew they had to be in bed by seven thirty and would see to themselves.

Jo loved to spend time with Nanna Mary. She had raised fifteen children, and the youngest was a year younger than Jo, which helped her feel like one of the family. She was friends with Dorothy, who was eighteen months older than her, even before Jim had moved in.

'Nanna, have you heard from the hospital yet? How is my granddad?' Joanna was crying.

'Now, love, come here. Don't get so upset. I will make us a cup of tea, then we will have a chat.' As usual, Nana remained calm. She never let anyone see what she was feeling inside.

Having had fifteen children may have influenced her appearance, of being overweight, but to the children, she looked cuddly, maybe because she always had cuddles to give away. Her bright blue eyes sparkled brightly, and her grey hair always looked as if she hadn't time to dress it, probably true, and also because one of her nine daughters would give her a Toni home perm when they thought she needed it. They sat on the settee together, and she gave Jo a big hug as she explained what had happened.

'Your granddad has had what is called a stroke. Have you heard of this?'

Jo nodded, too afraid to speak in case she burst into tears. Malc and Lynne sat on the floor near Nanna's feet, while, as usual, Harry did what he wanted, caring about no one.

'Well', Nanna continued, 'he is proper poorly just now, but the doctors say he will improve over the next few days. The main thing, Jo, is he will never be as he was.' The children pulled closer to her. 'He will be paralysed down his right-hand side, and his speech could be affected.'

Joanna was quietly crying. Nanna cuddled her even closer.

'Now listen, love, you must try to pull yourself together a little. Our Beth is coming around to take you to the hospital, and then you are going to stay with your other Nanna for a while to keep her company until he comes out of hospital.'

Joanna was ashamed because she was smiling inside at going to her nanna's.

She sat on the floor while Nanna Mary tried to brush her hair.

'Eh, you have a smashing head of hair, though what it'll look like when I have finished I can't say. My lasses all have hair as straight as pump water. That's why they spend so much on perms.'

The tumbling cascade of auburn curls sprang through the brush, falling down to her waist.

After lovingly brushing it, Nanna collected some from the top and sides and gathered it up with a green ribbon, to match her dress.

'There you are, pretty. It will do your nanna and granddad a power of good to see you.'

'But Nanna, what about the other kids? Who will look after them?' Jo was worried.

'Eh, anyone would think you were their mammy. I am staying here until our Jim and your mam get home. There is enough of them in our house to see to themselves. And remember, after fifteen of my own, I can manage these blindfold. Now look, our Beth is here with our Dorothy. Beth will take you, and Dorothy will pack your bags and drop them off at your nanna's, so give me a hug and be on your way.'

She helped Jo into her coat and waved her off.

When she arrived at the ward, it was a shock. Granddad had aged so much in the two days since she had seen him, but when he saw her, he gave a big, albeit lopsided, grin and held out his left arm for her to have a hug. That felt so good. He may look ill, but he was still her granddad. Nanna smiled at her, and said, 'Don't worry, love. He will get better, and it will be good to have you stay with me.'

Mum's face could have frozen fire. She was obviously very angry.

'Yes, you will both be fine. What about me and mine?' she grumbled.

'That is the point, Val. They are yours, not Joanna's, and if you care so little for your father's health, you might as well clear off.'

Vera looked at her father, and she was clearly sorry.

'I am sorry, Dad. You know I get tired with that lot to look after. I don't mean to upset you, but I had better go. Mary thinks she can cope, but she is getting on, and hers are all almost grown up, and mine are a handful.'

'The three little ones are in bed, Mum, so she should be all right.' Joanna tried to reassure her.

'OK, but I will get off. Visiting time is almost over anyway. If I hurry I will catch the quarter to forty-one bus.' She kissed her dad, said goodbye to Joanna and her mum, and picked up her bag and left.

'I had better think about what time the forty-eight bus comes for us to catch, and there is a big bag of Granddad's work clothes. He was working on the ships when this happened.'

Nanna was worrying about carrying everything.

'It's sorted, Nan. Beth is looking at a magazine and having a smoke while she waits for us. She said we are on the same street so no point in us catching the bus.'

'Oh, aren't people good when you need them. Right, Ben, we are going. We will be back tomorrow, and I will bring your pyjamas so you don't have to wear the hospital's.' She gave him a hug and a quick peck on the cheek. Nanna would never kiss him in public.

Joanna did though. She gave him a big kiss and a hug. 'See you tomorrow, Granddad. You behave with these pretty nurses.'

He struggled but managed to say bye to them.

Chapter Seven

Granddad was in hospital for three months. He came home in February, which meant Jo and her nanna spent the Christmas day at the hospital. But they had a wonderful time. The staff even gave them their dinner. Her mum did invite them for their teas so that meant Jo saw her brothers and sisters. Dad had had a phone put in, so Pete rang them at home that night, which to Jo meant they had an almost perfect day, which would be better when Granddad came home. They spent Boxing Day at her auntie Madge's. Her cousin Jacqueline was a little older, but they had lots of fun together.

There were times when she felt so guilty. She was so happy at her nanna's. She had only had to face Jim twice when she had gone home to babysit, when one of Jim's family couldn't do it. Her guilt was because she knew if Granddad had not had the stroke, she would still be living at home.

He was walking with a stick very well. Nanna had to help him wash and dress, and Jo would cut up any food that he couldn't manage, so life was quite good.

They would all sit together in the front room, her grandparents on either side of the blazing coal fire, and Jo on the settee with one arm that let down so it looked like a chaise longue. The big red leather suite was so cosy, Jo could easily have slept on the settee. They all liked reading and would sit for hours with their noses buried in a book; a regular trip for her was to the library to change them.

They had a new television, and Granddad loved to watch snooker. Jo found this a bit boring as it was in black and white, so how could you tell which colour ball they had hit? The two names she heard most were men called Fred and Joe Davies; she wondered if you had to be called Davies to play snooker. One night as she was reading while the snooker was on, she laughed when the commentator said, 'He is going for the pink ball, and for those watching in black and white it is the one next to the blue.'

Sometimes Granddad would tell his stories. His speech was really good now. The stories were supposed to be true, but Jo now knew which was fiction, not like the ones he had told her when she was six years old.

The queen was visiting Hull. Jo's cousin Jacqueline had taken her in her wheelchair up to Hedon Road to see her drive by. When they got back, Jo was bursting with excitement.

'She waved at me. I was at the front and the queen waved at me' was all she could say.

'Well, you should have stayed here,' said Granddad. 'She came in our house.'

'Did she?' shouted Jo in her excitement. 'Why?'

'Well, it was like this, as the cars were passing the Mayberry pub, they pulled up on the corner here, and her man came and knocked on our door. He asked if the queen could use our toilet,' he smiled at the look of magic on the bairn's face.

'We said, yes of course, and Nan asked her if she would like a cuppa. She said she would love one. So I said if she was hungry, I could go to the chippie for her. She said yes, and she had heard of these things called patties that the fish shops in Hull made. "Could I please have one with some chips?" she asked. I said, "Of course," and she really enjoyed them, said thank you to us, and then went up Marfleet Lane to where you were waiting on Hedon Road.'

Jacqueline was turning scarlet, trying not to laugh. Nanna and Auntie Madge [Jacqueline's Mum] had gone into the bedroom to hide, but Joanna was unaware of this as she hung on to his every word. The issue was she had believed him until she was almost twelve years old when a friend called Valerie had said her granddad had lied, and they had got into a fight that Mum had broken up, and told Joanna that it wasn't a lie but just another of her dad's stories, and that he had told them even when Mum was little.

At least now she was old enough just to enjoy them but not take them seriously, although some may have been true, such as during the war they had a club on the corner of Escort Street, and a bomb had gone off quite near. Nanna had been in bed, and when Granddad had got to her, she was as usual under the covers and eiderdown. So she was unhurt but refused to get up until he found her corsets. Jo had laughed and was never sure about that one as Nanna always wore a lace up corset, which she said helped her back.

Nanna had told her about another time during the war. They had just come back from the air raid shelter when the sirens went off again. She had said she was going to bed, and Granddad had taken her mum and aunties to the shelter. Nanna realised how close the bombs were falling and tried to get out of the pub. As she reached the bar, she heard the screeching whistle of the doodle bug stop. She knew this meant it was coming down and dived under the snooker table. When the men had found her, after clearing the rubble, all she had was a few cuts and bruises. All around, the houses had been flattened, and fires were burning everywhere. Two families who had hidden in their cellars had been killed, but the spirit of the people could not be destroyed. And after all the fires had been put out and things had settled, the all clear had been sounded, and Nanna had said what a shame they had a cellar full of booze and no pub. This spurred the men, who dug down into the cellar, and a street party was held.

The three of them would sing some of the old songs like 'That Old Black Magic' and one of Granddad's very favourite 'Bless This House' while Joanna played the upright piano; she couldn't read music but could play a tune once she had heard it. The music teacher knew she could do this and could never understand why Joanna didn't do better at school, not knowing Jo didn't like drawing attention to herself out of doors

The staff didn't realise why she had to keep a low profile; she didn't do anything that would bring attention on herself.

Her essays were now all about her grandparents, and the English teacher tended to forget his worries, another big mistake.

Now her granddad was making such real improvements, they started to go out more. He would walk with his stick, but Jo would push his wheelchair just in case.

They loved going to the pier and watching the ferries going over to New Holland. Granddad had helped to build them when he was a young man, and he was so proud. As a treat, if it was a nice day, they would take the return trip for him to see the boat in action. He would love to sit in the area where he could watch the shiny driving arms controlling the paddles, then going downstairs to get a cup of tea and a bun. The ferry ran from the only railway station in the country without tracks as the ferries were owned by the railways.

On the way to the pier was the statue of King Billie [William of Orange] on horseback. Joanna was in awe of its size, and she always looked at it really hard. Nanna Mary had told her if she ever saw any stirrups, he would get off the horse and walk away.

All the little ones watched for years but the stirrups never appeared.

Life was wonderful. The summer passed by in blissful happiness; she was starting to look forward to her fifteenth birthday.

Joanna was unaware that her bubble was about to burst. She must have stood on a lot of cracks in the pavement at some time in her life!

Chapter Eight

When Jo rode her cycle home from school on the last day of the summer term, she was very pleased with herself. Her school report was very good. She was pleased about this because her mother had made her take shorthand and typing which she didn't want to do, but her marks were good anyway.

Joanna had wanted to transfer to Escort School at the top end of Hopewell Road where she could study for nursing, however mam had refused to let her, she thought shorthand and typing was a better choice than nursing.

She ran in the back door bursting to show Nanna her report. She stopped dead. Mum and Nanna were sitting at the table, looking really serious, and they had a lot of official-looking papers on the table.

'What's wrong? Why are you so serious?' She was really frightened and looked through into the living room to make sure Granddad was all right.

Nanna smiled and said, 'Sit down, love, and let us explain. Your dad has been to court. He wants you to go and stay with him for the summer.'

'No way. I am not going. He can't make me go.'

'Now hold on. Your mum got the papers four weeks ago, and she has been back to court to see what she could do, and it has been changed so you go for two weeks' holiday. That is good, isn't it? Peter will love having you there.'

Mam joined in. 'Think about it, Jo. Another holiday in Wales has to be better than a week in a caravan at Withernsea with us.'

'But it's not fair. I enjoy having a holiday with the little ones.'

'Jo, you can still come with us. We are going when you come home from Wales.'

'You don't want me. You never have. That's why you are doing this. You want me out of the way.' Jo was inconsolable.

'I do love you, Jo. You know me and your dad had our problems. You know I had been seeing Jim for a long time, and from Harold down belong to him. That is why I could not go with your dad to Wales. You have the wrong idea. I have always wanted you, but it was so hard with you in the wheelchair and the little ones to look after. If your nanna hadn't been there to help, I have no idea what would have happened.'

She had kept her head down throughout, but she now looked Jo in the face to judge her reaction.

Jo was stunned. Her mum had never talked to her like that.

'I am going to first shop for some bits. I will use your bike, Jo, so I won't be long. Please don't start shouting. Remember what the doctors have said about keeping your granddad quiet and avoiding stress.'

She put the new pot of tea on the table in front of them and took her coat off the back of the bedroom door. She came and gave Jo a kiss, and whispered, 'Give her a chance, love.'

When she left, Jo said, 'Come outside please. You do not want Granddad to hear what I am going to say.'

Mum followed her out. Jo was very angry, and this made her talk very quietly but very intently. She didn't even notice her favourite smell drifting off the pinks in the garden.

'Did you hear her? Give you a chance, she says!' All the years of stress had exploded like a 'fifth of November' firework.

'What chance have you ever given me? You love me. Don't make me laugh, but the joke is not on me.'

Mum tried to interrupt.

'No, you listen to me. I didn't interrupt you, so let me have my say,' her words poured out like rain running down the window pane.

'Where were you when I was little, when I was ill, when Nanna sat by my cot that she had put in front of the fire, nursing me through pneumonia and diphtheria, when she was arguing with the ambulance men who wanted to take me to the hospital in freezing fog, and she looked after me rather than risk the journey. You only wanted me when I was able to babysit or look after the kids for you. Oh, once you realised I was going to walk again then you wanted me. You never let me forget how much you hated my dad, and how it was my fault you married him because you were having me! Why do you think Pete went to Dad's? He knows you hate him because he is my dad's son, not your precious Jim's.' She carried on without giving her mum chance to speak. These things had to be said.

'My exercises. That you couldn't be bothered to do. I was eight, Mum, eight years old, and Jim started to do things to me, while he so-called exercised my legs! You ever think about how quickly I walked? Well, it was so he didn't have to touch me. I used to drag myself up on the chest of drawers to make my legs work, so he couldn't touch me where he shouldn't.'

Val never spoke, but the tears ran down her cheeks.

'Do you remember what happened when you came home early when I was twelve? Do you remember that night? I will never forget it. I was so relieved when I saw you coming in the door, you would stop him finally and help me. But, oh no, was I wrong! Do you remember what you did to me?! Did you know he was using me as he did you? The difference being, you were an adult and chose it, while I was a child and was terrified. Oh, Mam, try to think how much it hurt. I was a frightened little girl, and he was a man, doing terrible things to me.'

In a strange way, Jo was taking pleasure in hurting her mum, watching her shed tears of regret, albeit too little too late.

'He would tell me if you or anyone else found out what happened I would be taken away, and I would never see Nanna and Granddad again. Relieved that you were there, was I ever wrong. Picture it, Mum. There I was, on my knees with him, making me gag on that thing, and what did you do? Can you see it? I can all too clearly. You picked up his big leather belt and thrashed me. I thought you were going to hit him, not me! You almost killed me with that belt. Remember the time I had to take off school until I healed, but the scars in here will never heal.' She pointed to her heart and head.

'What do you think Nanna would do if she knew all this, eh? What would she do? I know she would feel for me, because unlike you, she loves me.'

'I know I did wrong, but it did stop him, didn't it?' Mum cried.

'Are you really that stupid? Or is that just what you want to think, to make you feel better. It never stopped. It just got worse. Whenever you weren't there, or even if you were asleep, he would come to my bedroom, or touch me in the kitchen or whichever room I was in. Even if any of the others came running in, he didn't stop.'

She stopped for a minute to take a breath.

'Why do you think I wore those tight jeans and baggy jumpers. You hated them, but I thought maybe if he couldn't see me under the jumpers he would leave me alone! Why do you think I have no friends? For one I thought they would be able to tell, and two, I dare not bring them home in case he fancied them as well. You have no idea how much I wanted him to stop. Do you know one day he was asleep in the fireside chair after he had raped me. I picked up the bread knife and stood over him, but I ran from the room crying because I couldn't do it. Do you know what hurts the most, that when Granddad had his stroke I was relieved! Because that meant I was coming back here to live, and that meant I would be free of him. I will feel guilty forever for thinking like that, so do not tell me any more of your lies. I will never believe you or trust you as long as I live.'

Joanna ran into the house and into her bedroom, which was off the kitchen so Granddad didn't hear her. There she threw herself onto the bed and sobbed her heart out. Some of this was the emotion of remembering the terrors, and from saying how she felt and getting everything out into the open.

Val stood up. She wanted to go to Jo, but she knew this would not be welcomed. However, she decided to try. She went into the bedroom and put her arm over Jo's shoulder. Jo didn't even notice she was there. She kept her arms around Jo, quietly crying with her, trying to think what she could do. She couldn't bring up the children on her own. She needed Jim, and she hadn't told anyone yet, but she was pregnant again. They cried together but not comforting each other, simply because they were in the same room.

Chapter Nine

Joanna had accepted her holiday in Wales. She actually felt better than she had in a long while. Telling Mum how she felt had helped, and now she was looking forward to this holiday.

Dad had remarried to a lady called Morag, and they had a little boy Daniel, who was eighteen months old. He was just like Jo and Pete. He had big brown eyes, with lashes that looked as if they could touch his eyebrows, and curly auburn hair. The Irish in them from Sam was obvious to everyone.

Joanna and Pete took him for long walks around Betws-Y-Coed near Llanrwst, where Dad had bought a beautiful three-bedroom cottage that had a thatched roof and nestled comfortably into the mountain side. Pete was sharing with Danny so Jo could have his bedroom.

Jo was fascinated by the old fire range that Morag cooked on, but the food that came out of it was beautiful.

They would ride on the Mountain Railway that ran over Snowdonia to Blaenau Ffestiniog; they would walk around there before taking the train home.

Jo loved the rugged mountains of Snowdonia, and walking was her favourite pastime. When Dad had taken a few days off work, he worked in the slate shops, engraving slate for door signs etc. and was also a part-time guide down the slate mines. They would all go for long walks, and Jo would help Morag make up a picnic.

Morag was a really nice person, and it was very obvious just how happy the four of them were, living here.

Sam and Morag were concerned about Jo's reluctance to talk about herself, and they thought it must be because she had just met Morag and was finding things a little strange.

Joanna had thought about telling her dad but didn't because he would have refused to let her go home, and she couldn't risk being away from her grandparents.

They had gone back to Beau Maris. Jo had wonderful memories of her last holiday here, and it didn't disappoint her this time either.

Although she hadn't travelled much, Jo believed these must be the best sights anywhere in the world.

Gracious Regency and Georgian houses standing as reminders of the days when Beau Maris had been the home of Anglesey's gentry, and although it was in Wales, Jo felt it had an English feel to it. She read guide books and went to the library to find out more about its history.

She wrote all about the castle in an essay for school as part of her homework, how it is noted for its complex defences, designed by James of St George, military architect of Edward I. These included a moat and drawbridge, portcullises, towers, inner and outer walls, and around 300 places where the archers could fire their arrows. And it was purely the lack of funds that prevented the walls from being higher and the castle from having more defences.

Jo sat in what is now the magistrate's court, open to the public because it is not in session all of the time.

While she sat there, she wrote to her granddad. She knew he would be fascinated by all of this. He loved history and finding out about places.

This courthouse, she wrote, is in Beau Maris [beautiful marsh] and it was built in the early seventeenth century, and the assizes are still held here, and it is the only courthouse in Great Britain where the jury sat higher that the judge. I'll bet he didn't like that. Beau Maris is now a major yachting centre, and I am so lucky to be here yet again. It is the annual fortnight. You would love it, Granddad. I wish you could sit on the Marina with me; it is a wonderful site to see, with hundreds of colourful yachts criss-crossing the straits and nearby Conwy bay. You would love it here, but it is very hilly and you might find it hard to walk. Maybe we could arrange for you to come when my dad is around to help.

There was no harm in daydreaming, and Jo relished the thought of how she would love her grandparents to share this with her.

Dad had taken them down the slate mines where he worked. She was intrigued with how the men had worked down here. It must have been so hard for them; they had only been paid a few pennies, and this involved working with dynamite and digging slate out with picks. Safety was never considered, or at least not then. They worked by candlelight, and they had to buy the candles out of their paltry pay, so they would work in total darkness whenever they could. Dad turned off his artificial candle that he had brought with him, to show them what this would have been like. He held her hand because he knew she was afraid of the dark, but even so it was very frightening.

Joanna swore she would not be afraid again as it could never be as dark as it was down there.

The two weeks passed very quickly. Everyone had a great time. She had become very attached to Danny. Dad had promised her she could come back as often as she wanted to, and Pete begged her to come again very soon. Dad had told her he was sorry to have gone to court over this visit, but he knew she would not have come if he hadn't. He hoped she would return of her own accord. He even said she could bring Harold or Malcolm with her if Mum let her, because although they weren't his, he had been their 'Dad'.

As the train pulled out of Rhyl Station, they all waved and secretly hoped she would be back soon.

Chapter Ten

Nanna was waiting for her in Paragon Station, as Joanna knew she would be. After hugging and kissing, they went for a cup of tea in the station cafe before going home. They sat down with a tea for Nanna and a strawberry milkshake for Jo.

As Nanna was lighting a cigarette, Jo was looking at her, and she instinctively knew something was wrong.

'What's wrong, Nan? Is it Granddad?' she asked.

'No, love, he is fine. It's your mum.'

Jo panicked; she knew what was coming.

'I am not going back there. That's it, isn't it? She wants me back. I am not going. She can't make me go. Please, Nanna,' she pleaded.

The tears poured down her face. Her shouting was drowned out by the station announcer over the loudspeaker. Joanna was distraught her world had come crashing down around her.

'Look, love, I have tried everything, but your mum is adamant, and nothing anyone can say will change her mind. The problem is she is pregnant again. This one is due in January.'

'Another one! What is wrong with her? That makes nine altogether, and she is not interested in Pete. I can understand that, but what about the twins she never bothers with them and they are Jim's, all she wants is a nursemaid

'Oh, Jo, don't say things like that. She loves you all, just in different ways. The fathers of the children don't make any difference. You are all hers, remember that.'

'Oh, you have no idea how much I do regret that. I wish I wasn't hers. I wish you were my mam. When Granddad gets muddled and calls you my mam, I wish with all my heart that was true.'

'Listen, love, this time will be different. Your mum has cried her heart out over how she has treated you. She has promised she will try harder and make things different for you. So you must try as well. Try to meet her halfway. Promise me you will try, please, Jo. And I will pop over every day to see you, and I have told her you are to come and stay with us on the weekends when Jim is at home. So please, Jo, try.'

'It looks as if I have no choice. If I had known this, I might have stayed with my dad.' She could have bitten her tongue out when she saw the look on her nanna's face.

'I am sorry, Nanna. I didn't mean that. I will never leave you. You know that. You know how much I love you both.'

'Don't take on so much, love. I know it is because you are upset. You will have to tell us all about your holiday at the weekend, when we have calmed down a bit. And your granddad wants to hear all about it. He really enjoyed your letters.' She picked up Jo's case.

'You are staying with us tonight and then going to your mum's tomorrow. If we hurry, we will catch the 48. Look, it has just pulled in.' They hurried out of the cafe and caught their bus.

'That's better, and I have your favourite in the oven, savoury ducks. And Nanna Mary has sent over some of her scones.'

Things settled down for the ride home.

They got off the bus in Portobella Street and called in at Mackmans Cake Shop for some blackcurrant slices. They all loved them.

Chapter Eleven

Life settled into the old routine—seeing to the kids in the mornings before she went to school, getting the older ones off to school, and giving the little ones their breakfast. She would then wake her mum with a cup of tea before she left.

The big difference was that Jim seemed to have decided to leave her alone.

Harold was still a spoilt brat. Jo told him so many times, but he just ignored her.

He was supposed to go to Greatfield Secondary Modern School, which was on their estate, but friends of hers told her he was not going to school, unbeknown to her mam.

When she found out, she had talked to Harry, and he had told he would go to school every day from now.

His promises were like drifting sands, as he did not go. Jo knew he was pinching milk off doorsteps. He didn't even drink it, and he just smashed the bottles into the gutters.

After several visits by the 'kid catcher', he was taken into care in the home for wayward children up Marfleet Lane at the back of Nanna's house.

Mum was devastated, and she and Jim argued long into the night. He said it was all her fault because she had let him get away with 'blue bloody murder'.

Mum cried that he was wrong. She loved Harry and had done everything she could for him. Jim had replied, 'It's a bloody good job you haven't loved the others in the same way then, or we would have none of them here.'

After several tries by Mum, Harry was allowed to come home after three months.

Eventually on 15 December, when he was twelve years old, he was taken to court for shoplifting cigarettes, matches, and sweets, and being abusive and aggressive to the shopkeeper when he caught him, the result being he was taken to a secure unit until her reached the age of sixteen. He was classed as 'beyond the care and control of his parents'.

Even then Mum swore he wasn't a bad boy. He was just trying to get Christmas presents for everyone. She would always be blind to his faults.

Christmas was uneventful; it just came and went. Mum was still working at Goat and Compass but was leaving after New Year as she was so big with this baby.

Jim went for a drink most nights, so Jo was in babysitting.

Nanna did visit quite a lot, but Granddad had had Asian flu, and it was taking him a while to recover from it so she had to look after him.

Mum's temper had gotten worse since Harry went away, and even more so when the manager at the home asked her not to visit for a few weeks. They thought he was jealous of the baby she was having, and he would be out of control after she had visited. This really upset her.

All the older family members could not believe how one child out of eight could be treated so differently.

At the end of January, when the midwife came to visit, she told Val she could not have this one at home like the others. Jo heard Mum crying and went into the lounge to see what was wrong.

'I have to go into Hedon Road to have this one for some reason. I had the rest at home, so why is this one so different'?

The nurse replied, 'You are not twenty-one anymore, and having a baby at thirty-nine is not easy. Before you say it, I know you were thirty-six when you had John, but this one is breach and two weeks overdue. I am taking you in today, so Joanna can get your case for you. You can ring your husband and your mum if you want.'

'But what about the others. I have them to look after.'

'Joanna does a good job with them, so she can manage.'

Her mum stood in front of the fire with her hands on her hips looking quite scary. Jo was amazed at how the midwife stood her ground.

'We will be fine, Mum. You have to think of yourself and this baby.'

'But what about your O levels? You can't take time off school. They will not be happy.'

'Mr Innes knows you are due any day, and he said he would understand if I had to have time off. He said he trusts me to study at home. If I go in, they will give me things to do at home, so don't worry.'

The midwife decided she had to be blunt her kid gloves would not work.

'Mrs Wilkinson, stop being silly and think for a minute. Do you want to lose this baby, or even worse lose your own life?! What will happen to the other children then?'

The door burst open, and the twins came running in to their mum.

'Mammy, we don't want you to die,' they cried in unison. They often spoke together or finished each other's sentences.

They were hugging Val's legs; Jo pulled them away so Mum could sit down to give them a hug.

'I am not going to die. Whatever gave you that idea?'

Barbara said, 'Our Jo left the door open a bit.'

'And we were listening,' finished Patricia.

'I promise I will not die, but that means I will have to go to hospital to have the new baby. Our Jo will have to look after you all. So will you help her?'

Babs was excited about helping and said, 'Yes, we can help. We can even dry the dishes,' and then the two of them together 'without breaking any.'

'OK then, you go and play outside while I ring your dad and get ready to go.' She hugged them both.

The midwife was laughing. 'How do you tell them apart?'

'It's not easy, but when they are talking, Babs always starts first. She is the stronger natured and that helps.'

They left for the hospital; Nanna came to make sure Jo was all right.

Jim went to the hospital that night and came home at 11.00 p.m. to tell them they had another boy, but Mum had had a hard time with him, and they had decided she should be sterilised so there would be no more.

'Not before time,' said Jo. 'We have enough to cope with now.'

Jim agreed with her. 'Where are the others?'

'Malc and Lynn are at Nanna Mary's. The twins and John are fast asleep. I'll put the kettle on and make you a cuppa.'

'Don't bother with that. I need my bed.'

'OK, sees you in the morning. I am just going to do the packed lunches and then I will go to bed,' Jo said heading for the kitchen.

He took her hand and said

'Oh no, madam, you are coming with me. I haven't been able to get near your mum for weeks, and I need it really bad. It should be even better now. You are a bit older.' He was dragging her up the stairs.

'Please, Jim, no. Please, not again.' He pushed her up the stairs by thumping her in the back.

'Stop your whining. You are taking your mum's place for the next two weeks and then whenever I can after that. And don't think of telling anyone. Remember where that brat Harry is. You can soon be put in the same place, you know.' He threw her onto the bed and the nightmare became worse than ever.

Chapter Twelve

Jim rose early the next morning. He fed and dressed the little ones, put them all in the big grey twin pram that Nanna Mary had used for her twins, Jim and his brother Brian. He shouted up to Joanna.

'I am going to leave these at my mam's while I go to see your mam and the new baby. Then I will bring them all home with me, so get yourself sorted before I get back.'

Jo knew this meant she had about two hours; she lowered herself very gently into a really hot bath, although she wasn't really aware of how hot the water was.

She scrubbed herself with the loofah that was there, and she kept going until she had to stop because her skin was sore. She was trying to scrub away the memories of last night. He had used and abused her repeatedly, reopening all the old scars from within her memories, scars she had tried very hard to forget.

Her mind was in absolute torment, trying to decide what she should do. Killing herself had even been one thought, but she was neither brave enough nor did she know of an effective painless way to do it. Running away had been another, but where and what would she use for money? Who would look after the little ones? She loved them so much, and she knew her mother would never cope, and then what if he started on

Lynne or the twins because she wasn't there for him? And the biggest thing through all of this was if she ran away, she may never see Nanna and Granddad again, so until she thought of some way of escaping this nightmare she would have to stay.

After getting out of the bath and sitting at the dressing table, she looked at her reflection. Maybe if she could make herself dowdy, she could make him go off her. Jo never saw herself as attractive, but maybe he did.

While she sat there, she had been brushing her hair. Maybe this is what he likes. Everyone comments on my hair. Everyone says how beautiful it is. As she brushed it the curls tumbled down to her waist.

Perhaps if I plait it and wind it into a bun, he might stop. No, I can't plait it. Nanna wouldn't like it. She says it would spoil the waves and curls.

No, plaiting was out. *What can I do? Who can I talk to?* she thought. She felt as if her brain would explode with the thoughts fighting to get recognised.

The next thing she became aware of was that the dressing table was covered in hair and so was the floor; the scissors fell from her hand. And she looked at herself in the mirror; this girl looked nothing like the one who had been sitting there.

She heard the door open just as she had finished cleaning up the mess her hair had caused.

Her hair now reached just below her ears, and it was very uneven.

'What have you done?' cried Lynne. 'Dad, come and see what our Jo has done to her hair.'

The rest of the children had gathered in the doorway, and there were lots of oohs and aahs coming from that direction.

'What are you all staring at? It's my hair, and I want it short,' Jo shouted at them. 'Now get your coats off, and I will fix you something to eat.'

They all scurried away; they had never heard Jo shout at them before. Jim came in as they left.

'I don't know what you were thinking, but you had better get it put right. Go round to Brenda's at the end of the cul-de-sac. She is a hairdresser, and I saw her in the garden as we came past. See if she can perform miracles and make something out of what you have done,'

He left and went downstairs. Jo followed him, and as he was hanging his coat up, he handed her a ten shilling note.

'Here, tell her if this isn't enough, I will call in on the way back from the hospital and give her the rest, although heaven knows what I am going to tell your mam.'

As Jo went through the kitchen, he was opening tins of Beans and Spaghetti. He had bread under the grill for toast.

'Come on you lot, tell me who likes which.' And without looking at her, he said, 'Hurry up. I have to be at the hospital for seven, so you had better be quick.'

As Jo walked through the ten-foot alley way, she was thinking, *He hasn't looked at me once, so maybe it has worked.*

Brenda was twisting her head one way then another.

'You silly little girl, I thought you had more sense than this. If you wanted it cut, why didn't you come and see me. It will have to be an urchin cut. Tell your dad not to worry about the money. Why should he pay for a stupid kid like you. He has enough on his plate. How much pocket money do you get?'

'Half a crown,' Jo whispered, afraid to speak up and feeling embarrassed.

'Right then, you can pay me a shilling a week for four weeks to pay for this.'

When she had finished, they looked in the mirror together.

'Wow.' Jo was amazed. 'It looks great. Thank you, Brenda.'

'Yes, you are very lucky. It actually looks better than having it long. You are small featured, and it really suits you. You look very bonny, Joanna.'

Jo was walking home thinking to herself, *Well, that hasn't worked. It does look good short, and that is not what I wanted.*

Chapter Thirteen

Over the next few weeks, things carried on pretty much as normal. Jim came to her whenever they were alone or even if everyone else, including Mum, were asleep, or taking Luke for a walk.

Nanna had been really cross with her over her hair, but she did admit it suited her, and in any case it will grow back she had decided.

Mum as usual hadn't commented. She was too taken with Luke. It was a real shame for him. He was a lovely baby, but he had Down's syndrome, and Jo had got into many arguments with other kids who said he was Mongol, a horrible term that was used a lot.

Surprisingly, how Mum had been with her when she was in the wheelchair, she was the opposite with Luke. She doted on him and devoted most of her time to him. The old saying proved right: 'When you have a big family, they raise themselves.' The older kids learned quite young how to care for the babies.

Val had gone back to work at Goat and Compass, which meant Jo spent a lot of time babysitting, and which in turn meant once the others were asleep, Jim had a free rein.

When Luke was about eight months old, Jo realised she hadn't seen her monthly for a while. She couldn't remember for certain, but it must be two or three months, and she was feeling sick in the mornings.

She was terrified. *What if I am pregnant? What will I do?* she thought.

One morning, as she was getting dressed, her mother came into the bedroom. Jo was in her underwear, and she grabbed her dressing gown and held it against herself, trying to cover up.

'There's no need to do that. I know what is wrong! You're pregnant, aren't you? Don't try to deny it. You haven't asked for any Dr Whites for a couple of months. Whose is it, you dirty tart? Whose is it? Tell me!'

Jo was no longer afraid. What could be worse than this?

'Why don't you ask your husband? Did you really believe he was leaving me alone, especially when he couldn't come to you. At least that was his reasoning for what he has been doing to me.' Jo was surprisingly calm as she spoke to her mum.

Val sat on the bed. She had known the answer all along, but still didn't want to hear it. She thought Jo must be about four months by now. She was starting to show. She had known whose baby it was but didn't want her thoughts confirmed.

Jo never went anywhere to see other boys.

All sort of thoughts were fighting for space in her mind. Could she throw Jim out? No she needed him. How could she manage this lot on her own? His money was vital, but so was his company. Val also needed sex. And now that there was no danger of more kids, it was even better.

'Right lady, now here is what we are going to do. You are going away until it arrives, and then it will be adopted. I have already written to your auntie Sarah in Ireland, and you are going to stay with her until then.'

Jo was shocked. She had expected her mum to be angrier than this. She had known what Jim was doing and still wanted him, not Jo, and had been calm enough to make these plans.

'What about my dad, how do I know auntie Sarah will keep it a secret"

'I have already told him. I said you have been seeing a boy at school. He is disappointed in you but thinks we are doing the best for everyone.'

'What about Nanna and Granddad? I can't tell them.'

'There is no need. My mam knows Sarah is a widow. I will tell her she is not well, and now that your exams are finished, you are going to stay with her to help for a while. They need never know you are in the club.'

Chapter Fourteen

Life was so different in this part of Ireland; Larne is on the coast of Northern Ireland. Auntie Sarah had a bungalow her husband had built her before he died. It wasn't a big fancy place—two bedrooms, a lounge, bathroom, and kitchen—but very comfortable and homely. It had the most beautiful view of the harbour, and the seashore was about thirty yards from the front garden.

Her auntie was like Nanna in so far as she made all her own bread, especially soda bread, which Jo had never had before but loved it, and cooked good home-grown veggies from her garden. Life was very good, even with the strain of being pregnant and missing her grandparents and the little kids.

She had only rung her nanna once, because unbeknown to her, Mum had told them she had got pregnant by a boy at school, and their disappointment was all too obvious.

Auntie Sarah didn't talk about the baby as she thought this would help Jo cope when it was taken away from her.

It was very obvious who Jo looked like. She was definitely a Downie, with her colouring and curls.

The doctors had told her the baby was due around 30 November. What a sixteenth birthday present that would be! Jo's was on 14 November, the same day as Prince Charles, only she was two years older than him.

On the twentieth, Jo woke in the night in terrible pain. She called for her auntie, who called an ambulance, and they went to the hospital in Belfast.

At 7.20 a.m. she had a little girl. She saw her briefly, and she was beautiful with very auburn hair.

Jo never saw her again; the hospital said if she stayed in bed at home for another week, she could go home two days after the birth. The baby was left at the hospital. Jo had been advised not to even think of names, but secretly she called her Helen.

The social workers visited her two weeks later, and she signed the adoption forms.

Jo returned home on 14 December. Everything felt really strange, noisy and busy; she missed her auntie and especially yearned for Helen.

The hardest thing for her was earning her grandparents' respect all over again. Would she always have to pay for what he had done to her? By now she had stopped using his name. Somehow it helped in a small way.

Her mind would not let her forget Helen. She pined for her, and even her conception did not spoil how she felt about her child. She prayed whoever had adopted her loved her very much. Helen was her daughter even though she had never held her, fed her, or done any of the things mothers do.

Chapter Fifteen

The fact that she couldn't talk to anyone about her feelings made it worse. Everyone who knew about the baby [all the family], believed she had given herself to a boy at school. Dad said this was statutory rape as she had been under sixteen and tried to get her to tell him who it was so he could call the police. He was angry with Jo because she wouldn't give him a name; he had no idea why she couldn't.

When she visited her nanna, things were strained. Nanna had a hard time understanding what Jo had done. She put on a good front for Granddad as his health was not too good, and they did not want to stress him anymore. Therefore he knew nothing about any of it.

He did get easily confused; so much so he hadn't registered Jo had been missing for a few months. Maybe this was a good thing

Joanna's absence had been explained to the other children by telling them she had needed a long holiday after taking her exams, in which she achieved 'A' in typing, shorthand, English, Maths, German, and biology. No mean thing with all she had been going through.

Jo had got a job at Kingston Box Company off Cumberland Street. It was just up the road from Humber Pickle factory, and it took a while for her to get used to the smell, but then she didn't notice it.

She enjoyed her work. She had her own desk in the office along with three others, but hers was at the reception window, which was behind her, and on her left-hand side was the switchboard. Her job was to look after reception and the switchboard along with some typing work.

Joanna really enjoyed the work. She had control of the radio that played in the factory. She could stop it when she needed to make an announcement for someone to come to telephone or the reception. She would listen through her headphones. They could not have music in the office. Her favourite was workers' playtime. And another was family favourites that was always on when a lot of people, including Nanna, were having their Sunday lunch.

The only part of the job she didn't like was the way the office staff and factory staff had to be kept apart. She said it was snobbery even at lunch time. There was a dining room for staff, but the office staff had a small room off the main one, and they had table cloths on small tables instead of big tables and benches with no cloths. More over, after the meal, the factory staff would sit in the street, and some of them would play football in the street. Jo liked to play football and would join in. She was warned a couple of times about this but took no notice, until after four months she was sacked. The reason—she was fraternising with factory staff! She was terrified of going home and telling her mum this. She would never believe that meant playing football.

As she was sent from the office immediately without any notice, she went into town to see if she could find anything else; her luck was in. Asbestos, a sport and camping shop had a notice in the window for an office girl. She went in, was interviewed, and given the job. She was told she could start the next day and was offered £3 per week, which was ten shillings more than what she was earning at the factory. After paying her national insurance stamp, she would take home £2./15s/ 4d, up to now mum took £2 and she had 5 /4d, now she would have 15 / 4d.

She told Val she had heard about this new job and went for an interview, because it would be easier to get to being on the main bus route, instead of a twenty-five-minute walk after getting off the bus. Val said that that was fine by her, especially as she would now have another ten bob a week

Jo was disappointed at Val taking the extra money but knew better than to argue.

Her new job was good. She was in the office most of the time, but if it was busy in the store, she would work on the shop floor or in the cash office where the tubes came up with the bill and cash from the assistants; she would take the money and send the receipt stub and change back down the tubes.

The top floor where she would help out sold camping gear including tents and all the clothes children needed for scouting or girl guides, it was funny at times, like when a child zipped herself into an igloo tent, and they had a real problem getting her out, and a mother who brought a piece of string and said she needed a cub cap this size, holding out the string.

Jo had learnt how to talk to colleagues without really telling them anything about her life.

This time was different. She worked with a girl called Marylyn who lived on Village Gardens on Holderness Road.

Marylyn was a really nice girl who suffered from asthma and eczema. She also had a stepparent; hers was a stepmother, who was cruel to her, doing things like hiding her medicine cream that she had to put on her face straight after washing. The fact they had things in common sealed the bond between them, and neither would ever tell anyone what they knew about the other.

This made a big difference. Jo could now talk about her problems. She even told her about Helen. Marylyn helped her to see what kind of life Helen would have had if she had brought her home, and how much better she would be with her adoptive parents.

They would go out a couple of times a week dancing. They both loved going to Majestic Ballroom and to Kevin Ballroom, which was in the market square, so they could call at Carvers Fish Stall and get the best chips in Hull.

They also enjoyed looking at the history of Hull; it was primarily a fishing port in league with London and Liverpool. But long ago it was the largest fishing port in the country. It got its name in 1295 when Edward I acquired the land and called it King's Town upon the Hull, because it stood on the river Hull. This is why it is now called Kingston upon Hull. They would visit museums such as the Wilberforce Museum, named after William Wilberforce who was born in High Street. He was elected to Parliament at the age of twenty-one, and his fame was due to him succeeding to bring about the Slavery Abolition Act. He died a month before the act came in, but he knew he had succeeded, and the museum is a mine of history and information that fascinated the two girls. Another place they loved to go was to the Holy Trinity Church. This had survived the bombing of the Second World War. After London, Hull was the most bombed city. In the centre, 95 per cent was damaged, but the church stood proud. It is the largest parish church in England, and the oldest brick building that still serves its original purpose. They would be mesmerised by such a magnificent building and were delighted when they finally found the seven mice that Robert Thompson placed at the end of the pews he carved.

Life now had some good times in it, and Nanna was coming around. She had got over the first shock and admitted Jo would have had a completely different life if she had kept her, and Jo had promised her faithfully she would never let another boy do that to her until they were married.

A promise she knew she would have no trouble keeping; she never wanted another man near her.

Chapter Sixteen

Things at home had blown up big style. One day Malc came into the front room when the little kids where in bed, and Jo was babysitting.

'Jo, I need to know what is going on around here. And I want you to tell me the truth.'

'What do you mean? There is nothing going on.'

'Oh yes, there is. While you were away, Mam and Dad argued most of the time. The atmosphere was awful, then our Johnny asked me why you had gone away to have a baby. They had forgotten kids have ears no matter how young they are. And if it's true, where is the baby?'

He was so angry, in the half light from the TV lamp and the glow from the fire, he actually looked quite menacing. And although he was only ten, he was already five foot six inches tall. He stared at Jo, willing her to answer him.

She realised she must tell him something.

'Yes, Malc, I have had a baby. That's why I went to Ireland, and the grown-ups decided she had to be adopted, and I suppose they are right. How could I look after a baby? I didn't think I should tell you about it because Mum thought you were all too young, but I can see now she was wrong. I am sorry.'

By this time Jo was crying. All of the last year's emotions seem to pour out of her.

'I am sorry, Jo.' Malc sat on the chair arm and put his arm around her shoulders.

'I just knew something big had happened and wanted to know what it was. Who is the father and couldn't you have got married? You are sixteen.'

'I am so sorry, but there are things I can never tell you.'

'Don't give me that. You can't stop there. I have a right to know.'

Jo knew she would have to tell him something, but it couldn't be the truth, so crossing her fingers in the pocket of her skirt she said the first thing she could think of that was similar to what everyone but Mum and Jim thought.

'I can't tell you, cos he doesn't know. He is just a boy from school, and even if we would have got married, how would we have lived and where would we live?'

'I hear you, but I don't believe you. When do you ever have time to go out with any boy, and if that's true why were Mam and Dad arguing so much? And why is my dad ignoring you? He never speaks to you unless he has to. No, our Jo, I know you are still lying to me.'

Jo had been getting out of the rocking chair, but she sat back down with so much force it fell backwards into the sideboard behind it.

'No, I don't have to tell you anymore, and how do I know what they are arguing about when I wasn't even here? And remember, Jim isn't my dad, so he doesn't have to talk to me.'

She jumped up and ran from the room. She shared a bedroom with the little girls, so she knew he wouldn't follow her and risk waking them up. Jo got into bed and stayed there although she didn't sleep; she spent part of the night silently crying into her pillow and the remainder trying to work out how she could get out of this mess.

Over the next week or so, things remained strained between her and Malc, then he went away for two weeks on a camping trip with school, which she was pleased about as it would give her time to think what she could say to him.

The night he went, Mum was working. Lynne was at a sleepover, and the twins were staying at Nanna Mary's. She had laughed when she was getting them ready. They were chatting to each other, and Babs said, 'Do you think Ms Sellballs will come again, and we will have to hide again?'

Pat giggled and said she didn't know but hoped it was fun.

Jo asked them what they were talking about.

In unison they answered her, 'When we stayed at Nanna Mary's last time, that Mrs Selby who collects her provident cheque money came.' Babs continued, 'Well, Nanna calls her Ms sell-balls, and she said she had no money for her, so we had to play hiding. It was good fun.'

Jo laughed and thought Nanna will never change, but she is funny.

As Mum left for work, Jim said, 'I will come for a pint later. I want to do a bit of gardening first.'

When he went to the greenhouse, Jo bathed Johnny and Luke and put them to bed, tidied up, and then put the telly on to watch Emergency Ward 10. She loved Gill Browne. She thought she was a really good actress. She made you believe she was a nurse. That was on for half an hour, and then Jo had a bath.

Jo sat at the dressing table brushing her hair. It had grown and was almost touching her shoulders. She was daydreaming while she did this, when she suddenly became aware of someone else in the room. She opened her mouth to scream, but he was too quick for her and put his hand over her mouth.

'Don't give me that. You aren't afraid of me. I'll bet a bob you have been missing it as much as me. Now let's not wake the little ones. Come into our bedroom.' He was dragging her along with him.

He pushed her onto the bed.

'Now no screaming if I shift me hand. You know you wanted me. That's why you were sitting in your bra and knickers.' He moved his hand. 'Now come on, no screaming, or I will have to turn you over and smack your bottom.'

He was smiling as he said it. Jo thought he wanted her to scream so he could smack her, but she didn't understand why.

She lay there keeping very still and silent.

He removed her bra and knickers, and then started to gently fondle her breasts; Jo tried to talk him round.

'Please don't, Jim. What if I get pregnant again? What will we do then?'

He raised his head and looked at her.

'What if I want to give you another kid. You have just given away my daughter, and did it occur to you to ask what I thought about that. I might just want you to have another one.'

He took her nipple between his teeth and savagely chewed at it. While doing this he forced her legs apart and pushed his fingers into her. He then pulled away, and she prayed he would stop, but no. He then forced his thing into her mouth. She thought she would choke. After a couple of minutes, he stopped that and entered her. He looked up and saw her tears. He lifted his hand as if he would hit her. *Please do,* she thought, *then someone will know what you do to me.*

He must have thought the same because instead of hitting her he grabbed her breasts and twisted her nipple very hard. She wanted to cry out but was too frightened.

'Are you ready now? Here we go. You are going to have my kid. If not this time, then very soon.' He fell onto her.

As she lay there, she tried very hard to think of other things, but that was impossible. The physical pain was bad enough, but what really hurt was emotional. How could she get away from this? What could she do?

Why should she be the one to leave? She prayed he would go, even die; nothing could make up to her for what she was going through.

She eventually got back in the bath two hours later after he had gone to the pub. He had great pleasure in telling her he would come for her tomorrow night when the kids were in bed.

She was very sore and lowered herself very gently into the bath. She knew he was getting dangerous now, as if he didn't care anymore. He had abused her more than ever. Her breasts were bruised, her nipples bleeding, and between her legs was bruising and bleeding.

At this point, all Joanna wanted to do was die!

The following morning, she silently slid out of bed. She crept down the stairs to get dressed in the clothes she had hidden at the back of the cupboard under the stairs last night. Jo had no idea where she was going but knew she had to go. She had checked her purse and found 5s/3d in it, and she had also looked through Jim's pockets and drawers while he was out, and she had found another £6. That was nothing considering what he had done to her, so she took it.

Before leaving the house, she crept upstairs to have one last look at the little ones that were there, feeling sorry because she couldn't see Lynne or the twins, and knowing Malc would never forgive her for this.

She had hidden a note in his school bag, knowing he would find it first, telling him she was very sorry but she had to do this, and asking him to tell Lynne, Babs, and Pat how much she would always love them, but the memories of her baby tormented her and that was why she had to leave. She had her fingers crossed as she wrote it. Crossed fingers meant it wasn't a lie.

Johnny was fast asleep, but as she stroked his head, he stirred.

'Hush, my little pet, go back to sleep.' She kissed him, and he snuggled into his pillow and went to sleep.

Luke was sleeping soundly in his cot. He looked so cute, and Jo wished she could cuddle him.

She tried very hard not to think of Nanna and Granddad, as she may then decide not to go. She had written them a long letter giving lots of reasons, without the truth, trying to explain why she had to do this. She would post it later.

When she went downstairs, she had a drink of water and put some biscuits in her bag in case she got hungry later. At this time, she felt as if she would never be hungry again.

She felt as if she was in a horrible dream, walking around the sitting room, looking at the old brown leather settee and chairs, which had seen better days, that Mum had been wanting to replace but couldn't afford to. The china cabinet stood in the corner, and in pride of place was the decanter and glasses Mum's mates had bought her one Xmas.

That must have been the year the twins were born, because she remembered babysitting them and putting milk in the decanter and pretending to be posh, drinking it out of one of the glasses. It did look out of place as it was the only thing in pristine condition in the room.

Mum was very house proud, but with the furniture they had and all the babies, there was only so much she could do. She looked at the old enamel clock on the mantel piece. The bell had broken, so it was no good as an alarm clock. It had, therefore, been brought downstairs. Not that anyone needed an alarm clock. The babies would always wake you early.

It was nearly 7.00 a.m., and she heard a whimpering from upstairs. That will be Luke. Mum will be shouting for me to go and get him.

She collected her holdall with a few clothes in it and the eiderdown Nanna had made her years ago, covered in a carnation pattern on one side and old dance dresses on the other. Somehow she had managed to squash it into her bag.

As she walked down the street, she was looking over her shoulder wondering if she would ever return. That was a question no one could answer.

It was just as well she knew where she was walking as she kept looking back at the house.

When she reached the corner, she stood behind the familiar white telephone box. Hull was the only place in England with white ones.

Most of the street was still asleep, curtains drawn against the daylight, as she took one last look at their house. She saw the curtain move in her mother's bedroom. She squeezed herself behind the phone box and held her breath, hoping Mum couldn't see her.

As she strained to see through the glass, the curtain had dropped into place.

Joanna picked up her bag containing all she owned and walked away, with tears pouring down her face.

Chapter Seventeen

1965

It was only three and a half years since that fateful day when she had walked away from her mum's house. Joanna was looking out of the caravan window while she rocked her baby son on her shoulder.

The site was pretty. The gardens were well maintained, and a lot of the people living in the caravans had put colourful flower pots around, which really did look nice. Beyond the site was fields of veg growing, very popular in the flat landscapes of Lincolnshire. And as their caravan was right at the back of the site, she could look over the fields. In fact she and Ann, a neighbour, who was like Jo, always short of money, would go out into these fields late at night and dig up potatoes and veg to eat. It was difficult by torchlight, and one night they thought they had dug up a few swedes, but when they got back, they found out it had been sugar beet. Their husbands thought this was hysterical. But it never occurred to them to buy some food, instead of their wives digging around fields in the dark, late at night.

What did I ever do to be treated like this? Maybe it was my fault. I jumped in too quickly. And not only that, she missed her brothers and sisters very much. Baby Luke would be five years old by now, and Malc would soon be leaving school. Harold had been released from the home, but he had signed up as a cabin boy in the Merchant Navy.

Mum hadn't wanted to know her at first. When she rang the house, Mum called her an ungrateful little bitch, like she had forgotten why Jo left. This in itself didn't bother her, but she had wanted to talk to her brothers and sisters, but Mum would not even tell them she had rung, let alone allow her to talk to any of them.

She had written to Pete, telling him she was OK, married with a family and was happy. She had not told him where she was. Not yet, and she had things to work out first.

Nanna knew where she was, and they wrote to each other, but she had sworn Nanna to secrecy, and she knew Nanna was relieved to be in touch with her and would never tell a soul. In her last letter, Nanna had even mentioned Helen, although she didn't know her name and referred to her as the mistake! However, she had forgiven Jo for that and was happy to be in touch.

Jo had sent photos of her children who were fast asleep, one in the cot and the other in the pram just outside the door where she could see him. Ben was the double of his uncle Pete, and Gail was like Babs and Pat, but her blonde hair could also have been like her husband Roy's.

Tony was only three weeks old, but she already had the same auburn hair as Jo and Ben.

When she had left home that day, she had no idea where she was going. The train standing in Paragon Station had taken her to Blackpool.

She met an elderly lady on the train, who came over to ask if she was all right as she was crying and looked so alone.

She had told the old lady that she had lived in an orphanage and had been thrown out because she was too old to live there any longer; Jo had decided she would have no past to talk about.

Mrs Rooney had lived in Blackpool since she left Ireland twenty-five years ago, and she had a friend who was looking for staff for her hotel, and she would put in a good word for her, which meant she would have a job and a room.

Jo had started there the next day. It was a small hotel for Blackpool with just twenty-five rooms. Jo was a jack of all trades, looking after the reception, working in the office, and if they needed help, she would work with the housekeeping staff and clean the rooms. At least she had board and lodging as well as a small wage of £1/9/11. That was all hers. She even managed to save 10/—a week in the post office.

One night she went out with Josie, who worked there as a chambermaid. They went to a dance at the Tower ballroom, and this young man asked her to dance. His name was Roy Peterson, and although he was ten years older than her, he really charmed her, and they started dating.

Within three weeks, she had told him all about her past. He was so sympathetic. She fell in love with him. After three months, they got engaged, and three months later, she realised she was pregnant. On 3 May 1963, they were married. Jo was seventeen, and he was twenty-seven, but that did not matter then. It was a quiet register office wedding with Josie and her boyfriend, Bill, as witnesses. Then they had tea at the hotel with the owners Gladys and Joe Smyth and Mrs Rooney as special guests. She was so happy Roy only had a bedsit that was too small to have a baby in, so they had rented a caravan, knowing they would have to look again at the end of November as the site closed for the winter. Roy worked in an amusement arcade that also closed.

Jo worked until she was eight months pregnant, by which time she was massive and had trouble getting around. Gladys told her she could come back whenever she wanted, and she could even bring the baby with her. They appreciated how efficient she was, keeping the office up to date and looking after reception.

It was a cold night in November when she heard Roy's key in the lock. She knew by the way he fell through the door that he was drunk again.

'Roy, help me please. Call an ambulance. The baby is almost here,' she pleaded, even though she was terrified he would hit her again. He had been doing a lot of that since they were married, which worried her with being pregnant.

'You stupid cow, why didn't you call one earlier. My mates want to go clubbing, so I have only come home for some money,' he drawled.

'Roy, please, not now. I need you. The baby is coming very soon. The pain is awful,' Jo screamed out as another pain struck her

'Oh, OK, stop your whining. I will ring one from the phone box at the site entrance.' He took precious money from the housekeeping jar and left.

At least he had kept his word. An ambulance arrived a few minutes later, but she was not aware of a time she had ever felt pain like this.

The midwife admitted her, but told her she would be some time before the baby arrived. This was true. It took seventy hours of labour before she delivered.

The doctor came to the end of her couch.

'I don't recognise you. Have you been attending prenatal classes?' he asked.

'No, I couldn't. I live too far out and couldn't get here. What have I got? Is it all right?' she asked.

'No, I am so sorry. You have a little girl, but she has was dead when she was born, which is why your labour has been so long.

'Doctor, you had better come around here,' the midwife said.

He went to the other end and exclaimed, 'Mrs Peterson, push for all you are worth. There is another one.'

Jo tried but was so tired. In the finish, they had to use forceps to deliver another little girl.

'There you are. You can hold her for a minute, then she will have to go to special care for a day or so.' The midwife placed her daughter in her arms. Jo forgot for a while that she had lost a daughter, as she had the most beautiful baby in her arms.

'Why special care? Is she all right?'

'Yes, she is fine. It's just a precaution for all forceps babies.'

Roy came to see her the following day. He had been to the nursery and met his daughter. He was hooked. He came into the room bursting with pride, and he kissed Jo and told her what a clever girl she was, giving him the most beautiful daughter in the world.

Chapter Eighteen

For a short term, things really improved at home. He worshiped Gail. That name was his choice, but Jo liked it as well. He had made a display of all the things they had been given for her—little silver birth certificate holder, a silver mug, and others. The funniest thing for Jo was what an old auntie of his had given her, a silver sixpence as silver was meant to be lucky, and a bubbed egg as this was meant to bring good health. Jo had no idea what a bubbed egg was. Roy had explained that you pricked a hole in both ends of the egg and blew out the contents. He had bought a little silver egg cup to stand it in.

The bubble burst when Gail was only four weeks old. Her nan had told her that she couldn't let him touch her until after her postnatal check-up when the baby was six months old, but Roy had kept trying. He then lost patience, gave her a real beating, and took her on the caravan floor while Gail was crying outside in her pram.

Jo had packed her bags and gone to her mum's, who had come around by this time, although things were a little strained. However, when Roy rang and told her mum she was probably pregnant again, she went back to him as she had nowhere else to go. But Mum wouldn't let her stay with two babies, and Jim had been giving her those familiar looks.

Mam had told Roy he should be in the fields with the cows, that he had no morals and cared nothing for Jo. However, she still told Jo she had to go back to him as she had made her bed and should lie in it.

Roy had been offered a job on a farm in Lincolnshire. He took it because he had always loved working outdoors, and his granddad had been a farmer. They didn't get a house with the job, so they rented a caravan within walking distance.

This one was much bigger than the old one. It even had three bedrooms. Instead of buying cots, they had started off with a carry cot from the charity shop and one cot for Gail when Ben arrived. However, when they moved, Roy made two cot sides and fitted them to the beds in one of the bedrooms. Jo felt as if she was in clover, even with two small babies to care for.

Gail was the apple of her daddy's eye. If he was in at feeding time, he fed her with Jo's milk in a bottle, although she rarely offered to feed Ben. It was the normal arrangement for him to bath Gail, while Jo bathed Ben.

Jo was happy enough. She gave Ben all the attention time would allow, and she really appreciated the help Roy gave her. He would, although, still hit her if she didn't let him do what he wanted, so she learned to be very submissive.

The farmer and his wife, Tom and Emily Taylor, were Ben's godparents. They loved both the babies and had bought a beautiful Silver Cross pram. It was white with red hood and apron, and there was a beautiful rose patterned on each side, and a seat for Gail to sit on, although if the weather was bad, she could fit them both under the hood. Jo loved it and was so proud when she took the babies for a walk. There was even a tray underneath, where she could put her shopping, and the fact she had to walk four miles to the shops didn't seem a problem.

When Ben was five months old, Jo realised she had missed at least one period. Emily told her not to worry because you couldn't get pregnant while you were breast feeding. Jo was very worried she had breast fed Gail, there was only ten and a half months between her and Ben, maybe this was another 'old wives tale'; she didn't know how she would manage with another one. Ben had been difficult as he had an umbilical hernia, which had meant he had vomited after almost every feed. Her GP had taken him into hospital twice to give her chance to sleep for at least one night, and when he was four months old, they had operated to correct the hernia. They said he was young for the operation but as he was a big baby—he weighed eleven pounds four ounces at birth—they had done it, and he had never looked back. He was a really good baby, and the double of Jo.

She still worried about it. Roy had told her he would make sure she didn't get pregnant again. She wished she could afford the new birth control pill that had come out, but eight shillings a packet was too much. She could feed them for nearly three days on that.

Jo had to pay a visit to the doctors with a very heavy cold, which had gone to her chest and given her stomach cramps.

The doctor checked her over and told her he would give her antibiotic if she wanted to take the risk with being three months pregnant.

'Oh my god, the others are only fifteen and five months old. How will I cope?'

'That's all saying there is only one. You are quite big. This could be twins,' said the doctor.

When she told Roy, he had walked out of the caravan, and she hadn't seen him for two days. She daren't go to the farm to see if he was working. That could make him even angrier.

She prayed he would come back. She loved him so much, and he was a really good husband when he wasn't hitting her, and a brilliant father. She didn't take into account she had nothing to compare him with.

During those two days, she had cared for the babies but hadn't done anything for herself. Her hair was in need of washing and brushing. She had worn the same clothes for three days. The navy jumper had fluff off the nappies all over it, and it looked as if one of the babies had been sick over her shoulder. Gail did have a tummy upset, and Jo thought that was because she was missing her daddy.

On the third night, she had just put them both to bed when she heard Roy's key in the door.

'Roy, thank God you're all right. I have been so worried, I thought you had left me.'

She tried to hug him, but he pushed her away.

'Leave you! No, I can't do that because of Gail. Oh, I could leave you in an instant, but I can't live without my daughter. If I find a way of looking after her, I will be gone so fast you will not see it.'

He pushed her, and she fell and hit her back on the coffee table. As she lay there crying, the look on his face took her back to times best forgotten.

He started taking off his belt; she was terrified she thought he was going to hit her with it.

'Well, I don't have to be careful now, do I? I can screw you to my heart's content.'

He pushed her skirt up over her face

'That's better. I don't have to look at you. I can just do what I please.' He tore her pants off so hard, the elastic cut into her skin. In her mind she was in two places—here with Roy and back home with Jim.

After what seemed like hours but was probably only a few minutes, he was spent and rolled off her.

'Get in the bathroom and clean yourself up, you filthy whore.'

She was slow getting up as she was hurting. He lashed out and knocked her back on the floor, causing her to hit her head on the wood at the base of the bunks. He carried on lashing out and thumping her, especially around her body. All Jo could think about was the baby. What if he killed it?

He suddenly realised what he was doing and stopped. They both realised Gail was crying. Roy headed for the bedroom.

'You get yourself cleaned up, come on now!'

Jo sat in the tiny bath trying to wash her bruised and battered body. Her hips were bleeding where the elastic had cut her, and her eyes were already closing with the swelling and bruising. Her lips felt three times the size they should be. Her front tooth was broken, and she could feel the jagged edges with her tongue.

When she came out of the bathroom, he was sitting rocking Gail in his arms.

He looked up at her, and the shock was evident and obvious on his face.

'Oh, Jo, I am so sorry. I don't know what came over me. I am so worried about another mouth to feed, and five of us living in a caravan. Gail deserves better than this.'

Jo wasn't sure what to do, she didn't know how to handle this or what to say.

'I know I will go to the council offices again tomorrow, and tell them you are expecting again, and then they will move us up the list. We might even get keys to a house. That's it. That's what I will do.'

He put Gail back in her bed and then very gently helped Jo to bed. He was very considerate and really seemed to regret what he had done. As he tucked her in and kissed her goodnight, he said, 'In a few days when the swelling has gone down, you had better go to the dentist and get that tooth seen to, and at least that is free. They don't charge when you are pregnant nor until the kid's a year old, do they?'

Jo agreed with him, and he turned the light out. A few days later she went into early labour. The doctors admitted her to a gynaecology ward as the doctors said this would be classed as a miscarriage. She gave birth to twin girls who were taken away, and she never even saw them. The doctors said the babies were normal. Therefore it was probably the 'fall' she had had that had caused the miscarriage. That meant he had killed her three babies before they were born.

Chapter Nineteen

When Tony had fallen asleep in her arms, Jo put him into the carry cot and went outside to lift Ben out of the pram as he was awake.

'Hi, Jo, how's tricks?' It was her friend Shirley, who lived opposite her.

'Oh, I'm OK. Ben's had his sleep, and Gail will be awake anytime. Now the fun will start. Why do we encourage them to walk. They are easier to look after before then.'

She laughed and turned to the pram, hoping Shirley hadn't seen the fading bruises on her face.

'Here, give me them two. You go get Gail, and I will put the kettle on.'

Shirley carried Tony in the carry cot and walked Ben to her caravan.

Jo dabbed a bit of powder on her face, trying to hide the bruises, but she knew she was fooling no one. Everyone thought she was crazy for staying with him, but he did love her. He told her so, and he was always very sorry when he hit her. It was her fault for not doing things how he wanted. The main worry had been while she was pregnant. She had bled after a beating when she was three months gone, and he had also beaten her and sent her into labour. The baby and she had been critical. The doctors said this was because she had had a placenta previa. This had badly affected the baby, and they said he may not make it. What had upset Jo was that Roy never even visited them until Tony was five days old. They had christened him, and Roy didn't come. Jo was in intensive care and couldn't. The nurse who delivered him stood in for her. Jo decided then she would not let Roy have anything to do with Tony; he didn't deserve to.

However, by the time he was six months old Tony was a happy, contented baby, and Roy started to try and pay him attention so much so, in fact Gail was becoming very jealous. She would try to smack the baby, but Roy had realised this and tried hard to divide his time, planning things with Gail when the baby was asleep. That proved he was a good man, didn't it?! Even then Jo was still trying to limit his contact with Tony.

Jo still tried very hard to keep him away from Tony; he didn't deserve him after the way he was born, being so ill as a result of another beating that ended with her being thrown down the stairs, yet again.

While they drank their tea, they were watching Gail and Ben playing with Shirley's little boy Dean, in the fenced in run that Terry [Shirley's husband] had built for them. Jo had asked Roy to do the same, but he wouldn't as the council had told him. They would try to give them a house once the baby arrived.

'This is good. They get so bored in the caravan, and it is hard to keep them safe. They always go in opposite directions.'

'Why doesn't Roy make you a play run? It would use up his energies, and maybe then he would leave you alone. I'm sorry, Jo, but look at you. You haven't looked good since you gave birth, and there isn't a picking on you. How do you get the stamina to run around after these two all day, thinking of the baby and worrying about how he will be when he comes home?'

'I'm good. It is hard with three under three, but it will be easier next week. We have finally got a council house, and we are moving on Monday.'

'I am going to miss you, but you need a proper home with your family, and a garden for them to play in. I hope things get better for you. We are waiting for a council house, so who knows we may wind up living near you. Where is yours? We have asked for one on Ridding's Estate.'

'Wow, that is where ours is. It will be great if you get one there as well. I'll keep my finger crossed.'

'I am hoping we can have a break after we have moved. I really need to see my nanna and the younger kids. Miss them all.'

'You *know* if you ask Roy, he will let you go to your nanna's for a break. He would never try to stop that, because he tries to impress them, and you know she would help you.'

'Yes, I know she would, but I can't do that. She has her hands full with my granddad. He is getting worse, so I can't take these three to stay with her. Anyway she only has two bedrooms. No, I can't do that. In any case, I can't live in the same place as Jim.'

'Well, you should let your nanna tell Pete where you are. He would stop Roy's antics.'

'I can't. He is only eighteen. Roy would hurt him, and I don't want that to happen.'

Jo looked very wistful as she sighed, obviously deep in thought.

'I would love to see Pete again. I miss him so much. I miss them all. Did I tell you, our Harry, he has decided he doesn't like Harold, has left the Merchant Navy, and he is going to Trinity House Naval College in Hull. He wants to join the Royal Navy and make a career out of the sea. He loves it. I am pleased he has finally realised what he wants, and he is living at Nanna Mary's, and she will see him right.'

'What's Trinity House?' asked Shirley

'Oh, it is a college in Hull. It was originally set up in the eighteenth century and was the headquarters of the Guild of Pilots, who was responsible for the lightships on the river Humber. But it now looks after Marine Charities and is a navigational school, which is why our Harry wants to go there.'

'That's good news. At least he knows what he wants and is working to get it.' They were both relaxed, watching the little ones playing together.

She returned home and the children were all in bed. As usual, she had no idea where Roy was but hoped he wouldn't be drunk when he got home.

She was thinking about what the hospital had told her. She had some damage to her womb and would probably never have another child. They had expected her to be upset, when in fact she was thrilled. The way Roy was, she could have been pregnant again. Already he had started when the baby was only three weeks old.

It was lovely to see Ben happily playing. He seemed to know that he must be almost invisible when his dad was around. Roy had never hit him, and Jo would have left him if he did that, but he would shout at him, telling him to behave and shut up. Also he was noticing the little treats Gail got.

When Tony was trying to crawl and the other two were running around laughing and giggling, Roy started to get angry.

'Can't you shut them up. If you can't, I will,' he shouted at Jo, although he had never hit any of them.

She was afraid; it did seem as if he would hit the boys before too long.

Gathering up all three children, she took them out onto the grass to play. It was harder to watch them but less risky for Ben. Roy never blamed Gail for anything.

Jo could take the abuse herself but was really worried about the children, especially Ben.

It wasn't all bad. After he had hit her and hurt her badly, he would be really sorry and very nice to her for a while. It was just that 'the while' was getting shorter each time.

All of her friends from Blackpool had lost touch with her. Josie was working for Ellerman Wilson Line, on the pleasure cruises, and Emily and Molly had become memories. They had written to her, but Roy had taken the letters. And she was so ashamed of her life, she wouldn't write in case they tried to come and see her. Eventually, they stopped writing.

Where could she go with three bairns? Who could take her in? How could she earn a living to look after them? In any case, she knew he would never stop looking for her, to pay her back, and take the children away. He knew how much this would hurt her.

The following morning, she was trying to pack a few things while the children played.

Gail was a beautiful little girl. She had big brown eyes, surrounded by thick long lashes, her lovely thick hair falling in ringlets down to her shoulders. It was almost white with the summer sun. It was blowing in the wind, and Jo was thinking how hard it would be to brush it. Roy would not allow her to tie it up or cut it. This applied to her as well. Her hair was now well down her back, and the curls seemed to be stronger as it grew. The beautiful auburn curls in Gail's had golden highlights put there by the sun. She had only once tried to cut a little bit of it, and Roy had gone berserk. He said girls should look like girls and had said he would teach her a lesson she would never forget. After he had hit her, he would rape her. It was as if the violence excited him.

Jo didn't really feel the pain. She had grown up with it in one form or another, but now the worry of the bairns was really upsetting her. She would die before she let any of them feel the pain she had, or any other form of pain

Chapter Twenty

1969

Jo was rushing round the house. They had been given a council house three years ago. She was going to be late collecting the older two from school. She grabbed her coat, and taking hold of Tony's hand, ran out of the door.

Life had improved quite a lot. Having a house helped. They had three bedrooms. The boys shared one, and Gail had the box room. They even had a dining room. It was on a new estate called Ridding's in Ashby near Scunthorpe. It was back to front as the kitchen was at the front and the sitting room at the back. She loved it. The sitting room had French windows opening onto the back garden which was fenced in so the bairns were safe playing out there.

Roy had a new job, working for a building firm, earning a lot more than he had on the farm.

Jo was also working with a gang of women who were collected daily to work on farms, doing things like potato setting, picking and riddling, strawberry picking, screwing beet, and basically anything that needed doing on the farms. It was very hard manual work, but Jo had no choice. They worked Monday to Friday, from seven thirty to three, and they could take children with them. So all she had to do was drop the older two off at a neighbour's who would take them to school, and she was home to collect them. She also worked behind a bar at night. She didn't think about her days that started at 6.00 a.m. and finished at midnight. She had to do this to earn enough to pay the rent and feed them all, as Roy refused to give her money and she dared not argue. Jo had worked out that she needed £15 a week to pay rent bills and feed them all. When Roy was drunk and she would peep into his wallet, he always had at least fifty or sixty pounds in it. In fact, sometimes she would take a £10 note and hide it for use in emergencies. She knew when he was drunk he would have been throwing money around buying his so called 'friends' drinks. This was the only way he could have anyone to talk to in the pub.

Roy did not hit her as much now, but Jo knew that was because they lived near his mother who was a strong influence on him and had warned him what she would do if she ever found out that he had. Once, when he had hit her, he warned her not to go near his mam's until the bruises had gone. His mam had asked his brother Frank, who was younger but much stronger than him, to come and check on her. When he saw her bruises, he punched Roy in the face and warned him he would get more if he ever touched her again.

His mam understood. She had ten kids—seven boys and three girls—and her husband had hit her for years, but she couldn't go anywhere with all those kids, and he had eventually stopped. Roy and his brothers and sisters would laugh about how it was when they were young. As they saw their dad staggering from the pub, they would run and hide before they got a clout. Apparently, the best place was under the pram that was kept in the hallway, because it was a very tight space, and their dad couldn't get in there. This made Jo wonder if anyone had 'normal' childhoods, and maybe this was why Roy did what he did, and maybe he would stop soon.

Bill and Ivy had now been married for almost fifty years and seemed as happy as Larry.

It could be argued that as the fourth of ten children, he had grown up with violence, maybe he thought it was normal; His two older brothers had also hit their wives in the early years of their marriage and then stopped.

The other thing that had had a real influence on things was the fact that her friend Shirley, who had also moved to the same estate, had written to Pete, telling him where Jo lived and how she was living. She would post letters for Jo so getting his address had been easy.

Pete and his dad had come to see them. They were totally shocked at how Jo looked. Fortunately, she only had very small fading bruises but was so thin they were very worried. They fell in love with the children on the spot, and the bairns had really taken to Pete. Jo thought they could see how alike she and Pete were

At 6'3", a good five inches taller than Roy, Pete was very muscular, and of course Dad was no small man either. And Pete was only nineteen, twelve years younger than Roy. Typically with men who hit women, Roy was afraid of tackling other men. Therefore, he backed off a bit, and they had warned they would be back when he least expected it, and that if she had any injuries, they would give him double what he gave Jo.

All these things improved her life; it was not bliss, but a lot better than it had been.

On the way home from school, Gail was skipping and bouncing about as usual. She was never still, her long plaits bouncing with her. Roy had agreed as her hair was so long it could be plaited for school but must be brushed free for him coming home.

'Mammy, can we go to see Nanna Val and Grandpa Jim this weekend? Please, can we please, Mammy?' she pleaded.

As she bounced, she caught Tony who was threatening to hit her back. When he couldn't, he started crying.

'We will have to ask Daddy. He may want to do something else. Now sit down and behave. Tony, please stop that noise. She didn't hurt you that much.'

'I'll ask him tonight. He will let me go. He always says yes to me.'

Gail was almost talking to herself; she had already learned how to manipulate Roy.

Jo knew if Gail asked him, they would be going to Hull on Saturday. They would stay at her nanna's. Jo had agreed to get in touch with her mum following Nanna's pleading but refused to sleep there.

The bairns slept in the big bed in her old room at Nanna's, and she slept on the sofa.

The weekends were great because Roy knew that neither her nanna nor Mum liked him, so most of the time she went on her own.

Granddad had liked everyone. He could never see badly in people. One of his sayings was 'If you can't say something good about anyone, do not say anything at all.' And he had died in 1968. This really had crucified Jo. It was the first close relative she had lost, and the funeral really upset her. She hadn't liked sprinkling ashes on his coffin, and all she could think about that was they had left him on his own. Eventually, she started to believe his spirit wasn't in that hole in the ground, and she took comfort from the fact he had been on a trip to the pantomime with pensioners and underprivileged children. He had loved the pantomime, sitting with the bairns, and when he went to the toilet before getting on the bus, he had another major stroke and died instantly. This was a good way for him to go, happy and laughing, although it was hard on everyone else. But it had been on the cards for a long time. He would always have a special place in her heart.

Pete and her dad had also helped financially. She had opened a post office savings account where they would put what they could afford, and they had paying in slips which she gave them, and they would put money in there for her. Roy knew nothing about it. She had hidden her bank book in the lining of a box of rice in the back of the pantry, knowing Roy would never find it. The statements went to her dad's for safety.

Pete had a really good job in a solicitors office and worked part-time at the slate mine museum with their dad.

He had then gone to see his mam and Jim. He never told them what he had found when he visited Jo, but he did tell them that he knew they were somehow responsible for her leaving home and warned them if they didn't treat her right if and when she visited them, he would make it his life's work to find out what had happened.

Val and Jim both knew how close the two of them had always been, and they believed Pete could make Jo tell him about everything. And that would mean not only Jim going to prison but the shame of everyone finding out.

They had been very civil to Jo whenever she visited, and Val did seem especially proud of her grandchildren. They fully understood that Jo would not sleep at theirs, and never pushed it.

Harry was at sea a lot now with the Royal Navy and was doing very well for himself. He didn't come home very often. His new life was too important to him.

Malc worked in a local pub learning the trade as he wanted to run his own pub, which he and his wife Annette did when they got married in 1975 when they were expecting their first child, and they moved into their first pub in Hull.

Lynne was staying on at school to get her A levels. She wanted to go to university to become a teacher, which she did achieve. She married at twenty-four and moved to Sheffield to teach at a high school near her husband's family and his work, and then they moved to London.

Babs and Pat were heading different ways. Babs was studying at Escort High so she could become a nurse, and she qualified in 1972. Pat's hearing had gradually deteriorated until she was almost completely deaf. She learned sign language and studied hard until she became a teacher in a school for the hard of hearing, also in 1972.

Johnny at twelve was going to be everything, from a shipbuilder, soldier, train driver, and even a window cleaner, but eventually he settled on being a fireman, and Jo's kids adored him.

Luke was totally adorable and loving. He would never live on his own or hold down a job, but he didn't need to with his doting Mum and family.

Once when she was in Mum's back garden alone, Jim had tried to tell her he was sorry. He had never meant to hurt her. But he just couldn't help himself.

Jo glared at him, the hate leaping out of her eyes, and anyone there would have seen how much she hated him.

'You don't think your simpering apology will make any difference, do you?' her voice was low but menacing and filled with emotion, enjoying seeing him squirm, her feelings bursting out of her.

'I will never forgive or forget what you did to me, and I have never forgotten my daughter who I had to give away. Remember I am older and wiser now. I am already worried about our Pat, but I will make you a solemn promise. If I ever find out you are touching any of my sisters, I will go to the police, and I will tell everyone who really was the father of my first child. I will see you go to prison, and I hope they throw away the keys. I hate you, Jim, and I hope you rot in hell.'

This was never mentioned again, but Jo kept a careful watch. She had realised Pat was quiet because of her deafness, and Jo took sign language classes so she could talk to her, without Babs interpreting.

The only thing that was never discussed at her mam's or Nanna's was Pete coming out and admitting he was gay, and he moved in with his boyfriend Steve in a cottage in Rhyl, where Jo and the kids would visit them sometimes. Mam couldn't cope with this, and again she blamed Sam for everything. It took Nanna a while but she did come to accept everything, but on the occasions when Pete and Steve would visit her, she wouldn't let them sleep together, one always slept on the settee. Most of the time they stayed at Nanna Mary's who accepted everything without question.

So all in all, life had settled quite well. If Roy did hit her, it wasn't quite as often although he was careful to avoid her face and hit her on her body where the bruises couldn't be seen.

Jo had spoken the truth when she said she often thought about Helen. She couldn't do anything about it though even though she had always thought Auntie Sarah knew who had her. She also knew if this was the case, she would never tell.

Chapter Twenty-one

Roy was even being tender and caring when they made love. He said she grew more attractive with age. Could be she was not as thin and stressed out.

He was still very strict as far as her hair was concerned; she had managed to convince him that if she kept it at waist length, it would stay thicker and the curl would not fall out. He agreed for her but not Gail. He really had an issue with hair, and this was just one more of the ways he was unbalanced. Yes, things were easier to live with. However, Jo had no love or feelings left for him. They had been destroyed over the years, but she had to live with him for the sake of the children. Although she didn't blame her parents, she did think if they hadn't divorced, maybe life would have been better. So she was trying to keep her marriage together.

Her biggest fear was what would happen to them if they split up. He would never let her keep the children.

When Tony was five and at school, he brought a note home saying the nurse had found lice in his hair. Jo was distraught. How would she clean his hair. It was so thick and curly. What if Gail got them? Hers was even longer.

Her neighbour was a hairdresser, and she advised Jo to cut his hair very short so she could apply Prioderm and leave it on overnight and then go through it with a nit comb. Jo let her cut it, and also to thin Gail's out, trying to persuade herself she could explain this to Roy. It actually looked beautiful at shoulder length.

When Roy came home from work that night, Gail ran to show him her new hair. He went completely wild. His thoughts of what his mam, Frank, or Pete would do left his mind. He beat Jo very badly. She managed to run upstairs into the bathroom and bolted the door. He smashed it off its hinges. He dragged her onto the landing, thumped her in the face so hard, her two front teeth broke. He obviously hurt his hand, so he kicked her, and she fell downstairs.

Her foot caught on the wall as she fell, and she felt something snap in her leg. The pain was unbearable.

The children were all screaming; Ben had even tried to stop him and got a clout across his head for his trouble. As Jo landed in a heap at the bottom of the stairs, Gail jumped onto her and started shouting.

'Daddy, what are you doing? Stop it. I hate you.' She was very upset. This stopped Roy in his tracks, temporarily. Jo managed to crawl to the back door to get out of the house. This was hard as the pain in her leg was excruciating. Roy had been consoling Gail. When he realised what she was doing, he lost it again. Jo was cowering in a heap at the back door. Roy lifted the enamel bucket full of boiling water off the cooker. They had no immersion heater, so this was how she got hot water for washing up. As he went to throw it on her, Gail jumped on top of her mum. 'No, Daddy,' she screamed. Ben was hanging on to his leg, trying to stop him, and Tony was screaming with fear.

Roy saw Gail in the way and put the bucket down. He then saw the looks on the children's faces and realised he had gone too far.

'Oh, Jo, I am sorry. I just saw red. Gail, I didn't mean to hurt your mammy, and in any case, she fell down the stairs. Let me ring an ambulance, and we will all tell them Mammy fell downstairs.'

Even at this stage, he was still trying to manipulate them all. Jo was past caring. She just wanted the pain to go away.

Jo had broken her tibia and fibula just above the ankle, and it had been badly out of place. She had surgery to set the bone and was then in a pot for twelve weeks. The doctors also told her she had lost another baby. She was shocked she hadn't even realised she was pregnant, but then admitted she had believed she couldn't have any more. The doctors told her they had believed it to be unlikely but not impossible.

This meant she couldn't work, and they all suffered as Roy would not give her enough to compensate. She had to draw on some of her savings from the money Dad and Pete sent her. She had been saving it for a way out if she decided to go.

The children had to go to school on their own, which worried her, but Ben was sensible, and they were safe. He had seemed to grow up very quickly, and he was very protective of his siblings.

One day, the older two were at school, but Tony was at home with a bad cough. Jo had managed to hop around or use her crutches to do some housework.

She had just got herself comfortable with her leg on a stool, the pot being very heavy, when there was a knock at the door, and Tony opened the door and shouted through to Jo

'Mammy, there is a lady here who wants to talk to you.'

'Ask her to come in, love. I cannot get up again.'

A fairly attractive woman of about fortyish, with bleached blonde hair, and wearing a silver fox fur coat, came through with Tony.

'What can I do for you'? Jo asked

The woman looked ill at ease. She seemed mesmerised with Jo's leg and her fading bruises. Jo kept her hand over her mouth so the gap where her two front teeth had been could not be seen. She looked at Tony and said, 'This is very difficult,' she stammered, obviously very nervous.

Jo had a bad feeling but invited her to sit down.

'Don't worry about him. He is playing and won't take any notice of us.'

'OK, the reason I am here is Roy. I want to know why you won't give him a divorce. You live together as strangers, and so what's the point?'

Jo started laughing uncontrollably; she could not believe what she was hearing.

Tony had run in from the dining room wondering what was wrong with his mam.

The woman was shocked. She didn't understand what was going on. Roy had told her Jo was unbalanced and that was why he had to stay with her.

'I am sorry,' Jo pulled herself together. 'I have embarrassed you, although why I should be sorry I don't know. It's obvious you are having an affair with my wonderful husband, and if you want him, I will tie a big red ribbon round his horrible weapon, and you can have him.'

'Look, can we start again. My name is Myra, and yes, I have been seeing Roy for about three years now, and that is why I am here.'

Jo struggled to get up.

'Would you pass me my crutches, please. I am going to make some coffee, and then we will talk.'

'No, you keep your leg on the stool. If it's OK with you, I'll make the coffee. Where do you keep it?'

'It's in the cupboard above the cooker where you will find the kettle, and the milk is on the cold shelf in the pantry. We aren't posh enough to have a fridge or an electric kettle, or should I say he is too tight to buy them.'

Jo watched her take off the fur coat, wondering why she was wearing it as it was very warm today.

Jo asked Tony to open the French doors to let some air in and told him he could play outside in the back garden if he wanted.

While they drank their coffee, Myra had told Jo that Roy had promised to leave her but was afraid of what she would do to the children. And in any case, he had said she would never divorce him as she couldn't manage on her own.

Jo had started laughing again but managed to control it.

Myra continued. 'I need him to look after us. You see I have his child, a little boy. He is six months old now, but my husband left me when he realised I was pregnant. You see he was left unable to have children after a bad case of mumps when he was twenty-five, so he knew Christopher isn't his.'

She took out a packet of number 10 cigarettes and offered one to Jo.

'No thanks, I don't smoke, but you go ahead. Tony,' she called out, 'will you come in for a minute?'

Tony came to the door; he was impatient to get back out because he could play with all the toys when the others weren't around.

'Tony love, will you tell this lady how Mammy hurt her leg, and this time I want you to tell the truth, not the fib.'

Tony looked warily at Myra, who smiled at him.

Jo said, 'Tony, please don't be afraid. Daddy will never know about this, and you can get a couple of sweets out of the dish before you go back to play.'

Tony very sheepishly looked at his mammy and then at Myra.

'My daddy said I must never tell anyone what happened. He said we must say Mammy fell downstairs, but she didn't. He hit her hard, because I had to have my hair cut, and so did our Gail. Then he kicked her downstairs. She did have two black eyes. Our Ben said she looked as if she had been fighting Cassius Clay, whoever he is. I don't know him, but I do know it was Daddy. Our Ben is wrong, and she needs her two front teeth for Christmas, cos Daddy hurt his hand when he knocked them out. And when I grow up, I am going to kill my daddy cos he's always hurting my mummy. Is that OK, Mammy? Daddy won't know, will he?'

'No, darling, he will never know. You are a really good boy. Get some sweeties and go out to play in the back garden.' She was reeling at Tony wanting to kill his dad.

'I am sorry if that shocked you, but that is the truth about my wonderful husband. It's time you knew the man you are having an affair with. This has been going on since I married him eight years ago. He does nothing to contribute to our marriage. I keep me and the kids and pay the rent out of my wages for working as a farm ganger and a barmaid as well as raising the three children I had in three years, and we are suffering now because he won't help financially. I don't love him. In fact I loathe him, and would be eternally grateful to you if you can persuade him to leave me. I would be better off on the social. Tony wasn't lying to you. He had hair lice, and his sister's hair was past her bottom, so I had to have some cut off to treat it, and this is what he did to me for doing that.'

Myra stood up. She was attractive, and her dress and jewellery spelled money.

'I need a few minutes to think. Would you like another coffee?'

'Yes, please, you know where everything is. I am sorry I can't offer you a biscuit, but I can't afford any.'

Myra came back a few minutes later with two cups of coffee. Handing one to Joanna, she sat down. After taking a sip of her coffee, she said, 'Right, Joanna, I have given this some thought. And I have reached a decision. I know it hasn't taken long, but I always knew there was something not quite right about our relationship, and what he told me about you and the bairns. But never in my wildest dreams did I think it would be anything like this. To be honest, I simply thought he was playing me along in order to get what he wanted. Now I am not too badly fixed for cash. My husband just couldn't raise another man's bairn, but he left me quite well off, and pays regular maintenance. Basically he feels guilty because he couldn't give me a child. Anyway, I have the house which he pays for, so I don't need any support from Roy. Now I realise how lucky I was to have a husband like Bill, and who knows, maybe we can sort things out.' She stopped to blow her nose and to try and stop the tears.

'Now you, personally I think you are insane for staying with him, but that is your affair, and I know you have a great deal to think about. But if you ever change your mind, here's my address. If you need me to come to court to prove he has committed adultery, just contact me, and I will be there no matter what. Don't worry about Bill. He will have no problem with me helping you.'

They talked for a few more minutes. When they had finished their coffee, Myra got up, picked up her coat and bag, and she said, 'You stay there and rest your leg. Your foot looks swollen. Little Tony can come and see me out. After all, he did let me in. Will you do that, Tony?'

'Yes, and Mammy, can I see the lady go. She has a big car, and I won't leave the garden, promise.'

'OK, darling, but come straight back in. Thank you, Myra, and I will think about what you said. Take care.'

Myra left with Tony hanging on to her hand.

When he came running in a few minutes later, he was very excited, 'She has gone, and look what she gave me to give you.' He handed a bundle of money to Joanna, who could not believe her eyes. When she opened it, there were five £10 notes. She had never seen that much money in one go before. What was she to do? She couldn't catch her to give it back.

'Is it a lot, Mammy? The lady told me to tell you it was for you and not to tell Daddy. She also said she never wants it back. She said it was compen something for what she's done.'

'Yes, it is a lot darling. Do you mind not telling the others or Daddy? Can we keep it our secret?'

'Wow, me and you have our own secret. I won't tell a single person, I promise.' He gave Jo a hug and ran back out to play.

After thinking for some time, Jo got on her crutches and went upstairs with the money. She had glued a jigsaw to a board and mounted it on the bedroom wall; she slid the money behind it, knowing Roy would never find it there, and she would need it to pay the rent and bills, as well as buying food.

This safety blanket made her feel better; she had no idea what was going to happen as a result of today's meeting.

Chapter Twenty-two

Eight weeks passed by without any further problems. Jo's leg had healed very well and the hospital had taken the pot off that day. She walked with her leg straight, but they had told her she would soon be walking normally. She had to keep trying to bend it, and it would eventually bend normally.

Roy was especially late home that night. It had been a long day, and she was tired, but she knew if she was in bed when he came home, there would be trouble. This was another of his fads.

It was 2.30 a.m. when she heard his key in the door. She knew from the noise he was making that something was very wrong.

'Where are you, you bitch? I am going to show what happens when you open your big mouth and tell your lies. Where are you? You'd better not be in bed.'

He staggered into the room. She was terrified. She knew she had to humour him. Let him do whatever he wanted, and the bairns must not see any more violence.

He came into the room, grabbed her by the hair, and forced her to the ground.

'Unzip my pants. I need this so bad. Thanks to you, my lady friend won't give. So you are going to.'

She unzipped his trousers, and his thing jumped out already erect. He forced it into her mouth. He pulled her hair harder making her jump.

'You bitch. You bit me. Now you will pay for that.'

He threw her to the floor, kicking her in her back as she landed; he grabbed her by the hair again and thumped her in the mouth.

It was strange as while he was attacking her, the thing going through her mind was he hadn't even stopped to zip his trousers up.

The punches came thick and fast, the punches raining down on her like a hail storm. She was trying to crawl towards the kitchen thinking she must get out of the house; he would kill her at this rate.

'I should have known you'd be behind this. Myra has thrown me in, all because of your lies. Now you will pay for whatever you said to her. She was good to me. Now I am going to be so bad to you,' he was ranting as he hit her.

He stopped to light a cigarette, and she took her chance to try to get out. She tried to reach the back door, but she couldn't see for the blood running into her eyes. Then she fell over a chair he had kicked into the doorway. She hit the floor hard, and he was on top of her.

'Oh no, lady, I haven't finished with you yet.' He rolled her over onto her stomach. 'If you know what's good for you, you will get onto your knees.'

She did and felt him enter her from behind. It was very painful, but she daren't move.

When he finished, she tried again for the door. Just as she reached it, he thumped her hard in her back, and her world went black.

The noise had woken Anne next door, and she had looked at the clock, 3.00 a.m. She nudged Frank, 'Listen to that, Frank. This has been going on for some time. What should we do? It sounds as if he is killing her.'

At that point, there was a piercing scream that made them both jump.

'I'm calling the police' Anne jumped out of bed and headed for the telephone.

'You have called them before, and they can't do owt. What's the point'?

Anne was dialling 999 and ignored Frank.

'Hello, which service do you require?'

'Police please, urgently.'

'Hello, Police, can I help?'

'Yes, my name is Anne Gangell, 40 Manby Road. I am ringing about my neighbours at number 38, and he is attacking her.'

'We have been to this family before. There is nothing we can do. It is difficult with the law as it is around domestic arguments. Wow, I heard that. If you are complaining about the noise, I can send someone out.' Jo's screaming had been so piercingly loud.

'Oh yes, that's why I am ringing, to complain about the noise,' Anne cottoned on very quickly.

'Right, someone is on the way.'

'Thank you.' She put the phone down.

It was about ten minutes later that they heard the police sirens and watched from the little bedroom window to see what was happening.

'Well, love, at least they are doing something this time. The one you spoke to obviously cares.' Frank was heading downstairs. 'I don't know about you, but I need a cup of tea.'

Sergeant Browning was knocking on the door very loudly. The lights were on, but no one was answering the door.

'This is the police. Would you open the door?' he shouted to no avail.

He tried the door. It wasn't locked but wouldn't open. There was something behind it. He tried to see round the door, but all he could see was blood on the floor.

'Come on, lads, give me a hand. We have to get in here.'

The two constables with him helped. They pushed the door, while he had his arm round it trying to move whatever was there. He knew it was a person, and he was praying she was alive, guessing it was the young woman he had met before in similar circumstances. The slimmest of the three, a young constable, said, 'Hang on, Sarge. I think I can get through there.'

He gingerly squeezed through the gap. He gently moved Jo out of the way.

'Sarge, look at this. I think she is still alive.'

Jo was in a heap on the floor, and there was a big kitchen knife sticking out of her back.

They gently laid her on her side, putting one of their coats under her head. And trying hard not to disturb the knife, they had radioed for an ambulance.

'In here, Sarge,' one of the constables called from the sitting room.

Roy was sitting by the fire, smoking a cigarette.

'I knew you wouldn't be long. Did that Scottish bitch from next door ring you? I can count on her. Is she dead then? She ought to be, the lying bitch.'

Sergeant Browning was trying very hard to control his temper. He had never struck a prisoner yet, but this time was more tempted than ever.

Anne and Frank were drinking their tea, standing at the kitchen window, trying to see what was happening. They heard another siren.

'Oh my god, what's he done to her?' Anne cried out.

Before Frank could do anything, she was out of the door, her dressing gown billowing out behind her as she ran.

The sergeant met her at the door

'Is she all right?'

'Are you Mrs Gangell, the lady who rang me?'

'Yes, the name's Anne. How is Joanna?'

'No, I'm sorry, she is in a bad way. They are taking her to the hospital. There are three children in bed. We will be taking him to the station. Would you be able to look after the bairns?'

'Of course, will you take my number and let me know how she is? I will take the wee ones back to ours, and they can stay with me until their mammy comes home.'

The ambulance set of with lights flashing and with a constable on board. Anne and Frank had gathered up the children, and Roy hadn't liked that. He had demanded they leave his children where they were.

The police took him back into the sitting room, until they had gone. They then arrested Roy for assault, and grievous bodily harm. By what the sergeant had seen, he would have added rape, but a man could not be charged with raping his wife. Hopefully, one day the stupid law would change.

The sergeant checked with Anne that she had enough things for the bairns as the scene of crime officers would be coming in, and it would be a crime scene for a while, or longer if Joanna didn't make it.

Anne told them they would be fine. If they ran out of clothes, they could wear some of her wee ones. She was well aware they didn't have much anyway. She was more worried about their mammy, and would they please keep her informed.

Bill Browning found Joanna's mother and fathers' details before he left. He would ring them as soon as he got back to the station.

Before questioning Roy, he checked with the hospital and was told she was in a critical condition and was in theatre at that time having the knife removed and whatever else was needed.

He asked the Hull and the North Wales Rural police to go and tell her parents.

Roy was remanded in custody pending charges being brought against him; it could be anything from assault to murder.

Bill Browning visited the hospital regularly to check on her condition. Her injuries had been the following:

- Severe head trauma causing her to be unconscious for four days
- Multiple lacerations and bruises all over her body and face; both eyes were very bruised and swollen
- She had lost more teeth, and her lips were split and swollen
- There were obvious signs of rape, or would have been if she wasn't married to him
- The newly healed tibia and fibula had re-fractured

Even though she had all those injuries the one causing the most concern was

- Five broken ribs, one of which had penetrated her left lung, and the knife injury had penetrated the right lung causing bilateral Haemo-pneumothorax, which meant her lungs had collapsed, and she had blood in them. This was why she needed surgery to remove the knife, re-inflate her lungs and put tubes in that drained into big jars, to take the blood away.

Bill couldn't help thinking what a pretty woman she must be under all those bruises, and whatever compelled a man to do this to any woman.

He sat in the hospital corridor talking to Detective Paddy McGuire

'What will he be charged with, Paddy, do you know?'

'Not enough, Bill. The laws around domestic violence and domestic rape have to be changed and quick. Do you know he will probably walk with a fine and, maybe, probation?'

'Bloody hell.'

'The only way this will differ is if she doesn't make it, and even then he probably won't get life. A man has the right to do almost anything to his wife. I know a lot of the wives wouldn't press charges anyway but the law has to change.'

Chapter Twenty-three

Bill was walking up and down the corridor. Paddy told him he looked like an expectant husband.

'Let's hope she lets us prosecute when she wakes up.'

An auxiliary nurse came down the corridor to them.

'Sister says to tell you Mrs Peterson has come around, and you can see her for a few minutes.'

They thanked her, picked up their coats and followed her down the corridor to the intensive care unit.

They had moved her into a private room; they could see she was awake although she couldn't open her eyes.

They introduced themselves and sat at the side of her bed.

'Hello, love,' Paddy smiled. 'How are you feeling? It is good to see you awake.'

Jo had difficulty talking as her mouth was so swollen, but by listening carefully they could understand her. She also had a lisp where the teeth were missing. Her denture with the two teeth on had been broken in the attack, which made it worse.

'Where are my children? Are they all right?'

'They are staying with the Gangell's, and they are fine, so don't worry about them,' Bill assured her.

He put his hand on her arm to reassure her.

'When you look a bit better, we will bring them to see you. You just concentrate on getting well.'

'Can you remember what happened? Do you think you can talk about it?' asked Paddy.

'Yes, I can talk about it, but first, are you the one who got me out? The nurses said it was someone called Bill.'

'No, love, that was my mate here. You must be a special little lady. He has been in everyday to see you, along with your dad, and your brother Pete. Your mam's been a couple of times as well along with some of your in-laws.'

Jo turned her head towards Bill; she was obviously trying to see through the bruises.

'Thank you so much, especially for making sure the bairns were all right. He wouldn't touch my daughter, but I'm not so sure about my sons. Thank you.'

'You are more than welcome, love. I only wish we had got there sooner.'

'That's all right. You got there. That's all that matters.'

'Now then, let me see what I can remember. He was late home and that often means trouble, but this time was much worse. When he opened the door, I knew by his ranting this time was going to be bad. It turns out his ex-lady friend, who had been to see me a few weeks ago and decided she wanted no more to do with him, had told him they were finished, and he blamed me. I'm sorry I am confused and trying to put things in order.'

She reached for the tissues as her eyes were watering. Paddy handed her some and told her not to worry. She was doing really well. He was worried in case she moved or something. She had a drip in one arm, a catheter in and a big tube coming out of each lung, as well as the pot on her leg.

The machine that was measuring her heartbeat was jumping around like crazy.

A nurse came in and looked at Joanna and the heart monitor.

'Are you all right, love? Have you had enough for now?'

'No, I will feel better when I have told them what happened to me.'

The nurse said that was all right as long as she didn't get too upset and left the room.

'Right, colleen, now don't get upset. Just take your time. We can follow you.' Paddy's Irish brogue was reassuring

'My dad's from Newtownards, and my auntie lives in Larne. Do you know them places?'

'Well, now would I know them places. Sure, I am from Bally Walter, so I know them very well. In fact my ma's friend, who lives in Larne and plays golf with her, has hair the double of yours. Would your auntie be called Sarah O'Leary by any chance?'

'Yes, she is, fancy you knowing her!' she flinched with pain.

'Anyway, let me think where was I. Well, he beat me and kicked me, as well as doing other things. He always wants that when he hits me, like it turns him on or something. Anyway I kept trying and managed to get to the back door. Then I can't remember anything. The nurses tell me he stabbed me, but I can't remember that bit.'

Bill took her hand.

'Listen, Joanna, you have done very well tonight. We are going to leave you now and come back tomorrow. You get some rest. That will help you get better, then we can work out what to do next.'

'What about Roy? Where is he? He isn't going to come here, is he?'

'You don't need to worry about that. He is in custody, and if we have to release him, we will make sure you and your bairns are safe and sound. So Bill is right, you get some sleep, and we will see you tomorrow.'

Apart from the bruises, she was the colour of the crisp white pillows she lay on, and so thin, she looked as if she would break.

'Thank you for coming, and especially, thank you Bill for rescuing me. I will always be grateful.'

'You are more than welcome. Now look, here are the nurses to make you more comfortable. We will see you tomorrow.' They picked up their coats and left.

As they got into the car, Paddy lit his pipe and Bill a cigarette.

'That rotten evil bastard. I wish we could lock him up and throw away the key,' swore Bill

'I agree with you, but you know he will probably be out by tomorrow, don't you? And what do we do then. It is easy to protect that lovely young lady, but what about the bairns? Can we stop him from taking them? I aren't sure. I wish I was.'

'I had thought about that. We had better talk to the NSPC and the social workers to see what we can do if he takes them. That will break her heart more than all of this could ever do.'

They drove away thinking about everything. They had other things to think about as well. Frank Gangell was livid at what had happened, and what would her father and brother do if they ran into him? They would hate it if they had to charge any of them for giving him what he deserved.

Chapter Twenty-four

Malc pulled himself from his deep sleep. Who was hammering on the door? He looked at the clock. Four ten. 'What the.'

When he looked out of the window, he was surprised to see a police car outside. He started to panic, and he knew everyone was in bed. He shared with Johnny and Luke, and they were both fast asleep.

He went downstairs and opened the door.

'Is the Wilkinson's, sir?' asked one of the police.

'Yes, I am Malcolm. What happened?'

'Do you know Joanna Peterson?'

'Yes, come in.' He moved into the hallway. 'What's wrong? What has happened to her?'

'What relation are you?'

'I am her brother. Please tell me what is wrong.'

He turned on the front room light.

'The Scunthorpe police have asked us to come. Your sister has been hurt and is in the hospital there.'

'What do you mean hurt? Who hurt her and how bad is she?' Malc was getting angry now. He needed to know more.

'We can't tell you a great deal. Just that she is in a bad way. Your sister has been attacked by her husband and is quite badly injured.'

Malc marched up and down the room. He thumped the wall.

'I knew something like this would happen. Will they tell me anything if I ring up? No, probably not. I will get dressed and go there. I can use Dad's car. I am sorry, officer. I am rambling, aren't I? Just how bad is she?'

'Look, we can't tell you anymore, but if you ring this number and speak to Sergeant Browning, he is the officer involved, he will be able to tell you more. And, yes, a car would be better. It will take ages by ferry and bus, and the first ferry doesn't go until six forty-five.'

Malc thanked them and showed them out.

'Thank you, I will ring your colleague and then go to Scunthorpe.'

As he went back into the hallway, his mother was coming down the stairs tying her dressing gown.

'What is going on? Why are you up, and who was at the door?'

'It's our Jo, Mam, that bastard has beaten her so bad she is in hospital. I'm just gonna ring Scunthorpe police to find out how bad she is.'

'What has she done now to upset him like that?'

'Oh, Mam shut up. If you can't see it's not right for any man to do that for whatever reason, then shut up and put the kettle on. I'm gonna ring the police.'

Val knew he was very angry and decided not to argue. She headed into the kitchen to make the tea, while Malc headed for the telephone in the cubbyhole in the hall.

When he had finished the call, he came back and sat at the kitchen table. He was ashen and obviously very shocked and angry.

Val was opening the curtains. The rain had finally stopped, and the early morning sun was trying to break through.

'Well, are you going to tell me what's happened then?' she demanded.

'He's beaten her to a pulp, and if that isn't enough, he stuck a knife in her back. She is in theatre and is classed as critical. He has been arrested and is in the police station, and he had better stay there! Will kill him if

I ever set eyes on him again. Oh, and if you're interested, a neighbour has the bairns.'

'Don't talk stupid. What good will it do for you to hit him? Anyway, you don't know what she is like. You only think you do.'

'Oh yes I do know what she's like, her and our Pete, which is more than you can say. You never gave a damn about them two, did you? Now shut your mouth if you can't say anything better than that garbage.'

At that point, Jim came into the kitchen.

'What the hell's going on? Are you two trying to wake the whole house up?'

Malc told him what had happened.

'Bloody hell, the man must be mental. What could she do to warrant that? Poor kid.'

'I might have known you'd be on her side. That's only to be expected, isn't it?' Val was jealous, even when she was miles away, Jo could come between them.

Malc stood up and looked at the two of them.

'I reckon it's about time you two told me the truth. This house has been overflowing with secrets and lies for years. Come on tell me the truth.'

Val was now scared. He could never find out about Jim and Jo's baby, or what she could only guess had happened that night when Jo left home.

Malcolm wasn't daft. He knew Jo would never leave the little ones or her beloved Nanna unless she was desperate. Malc would never forgive his dad or her, and that meant he would tell Harry. They had become close. Harry had changed and was a good man. If Malc found out and told him, she would lose him forever, and she couldn't cope with that. Her mind was in turmoil. What could she do but carry on denying everything.

'Now who is getting fanciful ideas. She left cos she was rightly ashamed of herself after having that kid, especially with your nanna. Jo knew how much she had hurt her. She didn't think about how given time my mam would have forgiven her, like she has now. Jo stays there often enough. My mam always did let her get away with blue murder. Oh hell, who is gonna tell her what's happened. You know the doctors are worried about her heart and that angina. Maybe we should wait until Jo is better. Yes, that'll be best.'

Val was rambling, trying to think what she could say to pacify him.

Malc went upstairs, completely ignoring the two of them; he got dressed and came back downstairs.

'Right, will you ring the Crown for me. Tell them I will be taking a few days off. I am going to Nanna Mary's, and me and Harry will go to Scunthorpe in his car. And if you want to know how she is, you can make your own way there, but I will warn you now.' He was looking at his mother. 'You start with any of your rubbish and upset her, and I will personally throw you out of there, and by the way, once this is sorted, I want the truth out of one of you.'

He slammed the door, pushed his BSA Bantam from round the back, put on his helmet and left. He knew he couldn't ride all the way to Scunthorpe on his bike. It was an old one and not reliable enough. Fortunately, Harry was on leave, so he would go with him. Nanna Mary was very upset, but the lads reassured her and told her they would ring as soon as they knew anything. They also asked her to go over later and tell their other Nanna because their mam wouldn't, and she had a right to know. Mary agreed but said she would wait until they had rung her so she might know a bit more.

They climbed into Harry's MG midget and left.

Chapter Twenty-five

They had been very shocked and upset to see Jo looking the way she did. Harry wasn't as close to her as Malc, mainly because they didn't meet up that often, but he was shocked and angry that any man could do that to a woman. They agreed that they wouldn't have known it was her if the nurses hadn't told them which bed she was in. This sad little thing in the bed looked nothing like their beautiful sister.

They wanted to go and find him but were foiled there as the sergeant who had got Jo out of the house had told them he was still in custody.

They checked into the Station Hotel, as it was the nearest to the hospital. They rang both Nannas and told them as much as they could as Jo was still unconscious, but the doctors had said she was stable for now. Nanna Mary had suggested they bring the bairns back to hers, as she had more room than their other Nanna. And they all knew they couldn't go to their mam's. Jo would be upset if that happened, although they didn't know why.

Sergeant Browning had agreed that would be a good idea, because if Roy got out, he would go straight for them and that would put the Gangells in a difficult position.

They went back to see Jo that night and then took a walk to gather their thoughts. Scunthorpe was a depressing place, dark and surrounded by huge steelworks which cast a dirty haze over the whole area.

Harry fell asleep, and Malc lay there trying to, but he couldn't shut out the memories and thoughts flooding through his brain. Pete had arrived with his dad while they were at the hospital, and it had come down to the fact that there were now four very angry men who loved Jo and wanted to meet up with Roy.

They had been surprised when Roy's mam and three of his brothers, Paul, Terry, and Frank, had turned up at the hospital. They were obviously very fond of Jo and very angry at Roy. Ivy agreed the best place for the bairns was in Hull. She would take them but as long as they were in Scunthorpe, they could be in danger from her lunatic son.

Malc eventually drifted off, but in the next room where Sam and Pete were staying, Pete was not so lucky.

He lay on his bed fully dressed; he wanted to be able to get away quickly if the hospital rang.

Chapter Twenty-six

Pete lay on the bed thinking all sorts of things, especially thoughts of their childhood. Even when he was just three years old, he remember hearing Mam and Nanna talking about his sister coming home. He couldn't remember the words, but the excitement was still in his mind.

He didn't like having a sister who he could only see when Nanna took him to see her, and she was in a big bed that he had to be lifted onto it.

He remembered walking down those long, long corridors, and the walls being shiny dark green. Nanna had said they were tiles. He didn't care. He didn't like them, and the building smelt horrible. It was like when Mam had cleaned the toilet at home.

When he had gone home that night, he had been chattering about Jo, very excited because she was coming home. Mam had clouted him and told him to shut up about her. He did. Even at three years old, he knew what he should do.

When Jo had come home, she had stayed at Nanna's house, but that was just next door. So he could see her every day. They played for hours, looking at books, and Nanna teaching them the words. He hadn't learned many, but Jo did. They enjoyed colouring and playing cards. And he loved playing snap and fish the best.

Often they just sat together listening to the radio, although he knew his attention span hadn't been more than a few minutes. But you are given licence to change things in your memories.

He remembered very well when they would be around at Nanna's, she would cut the rhubarb in her garden and put some sugar in bread paper, and they would enjoy dipping the rhubarb and eating it. They would sit in the garden where the border down the side of the path was planted with pinks, and he would never forget the wonderful smell of them.

Nanna used to have the 'pop' man call every week, and she would buy Dandelion and Burdock, and Ginger beer, which they all enjoyed. She made her own lemonade which was absolutely delicious.

On a weekend or school holidays, Padgett's ice cream man would come. He would be inside the cart with the ice cream and a hook where he would fasten the reigns for the horse that pulled him round.

Nanna would give them a carrot for Charlie the horse, and the man would always put extra raspberry sauce on their cornets.

If only those days could have lasted for ever.

He remembers vividly the day when his mam told him Jo was coming home. She had been at Nanna's for so long, or so it seemed to him. He had heard his mam and Jim talking about moving house and bringing Jo home to help his mam. He wasn't sure why Mam needed her to help, but he didn't care he was so happy she was coming home.

'Hey, Pete, our Jo's coming down the street with Nanna,' Harry had shouted. He had run downstairs, falling over the boxes in the hall that hadn't been unpacked yet.

They had come in the back door, as he had bounced into the kitchen.

Jo was a bit wobbly on her calipers and the boots looked bigger than her.

She was very quiet and looked a bit upset. Pete had hoped it wasn't because she didn't want to stay.

He ran over to her.

'Jo, this is great. Come on upstairs, and I will show you your room and our room.' In his excitement, he tried to pull her by the hand, and she nearly fell. Luckily, Nanna caught her.

'Try to be a bit more careful, our Peter. Remember she needs time, and her crutches to walk with you.'

'I'm sorry, Jo. Are you all right?'

'Of course, I am. Just let me walk in my own time.' She laughed and followed him.

He had been so excited, trying to convince her that things would work out for them all, so much so she had started to look pleased to be there. There had been tell-tale signs that she had been crying. She had said everything was good. She was just going to miss Nanna and Granddad.

Their happiness had soured from that first night. He remembered hearing his mam go into Jo's room when they had gone to bed. It had sounded as if she was talking through her teeth, which meant she was angry. He knew better than to go in and suffer her wrath.

When she had left, he had heard Jo crying. He was afraid to go to her in case Mam heard him.

He vowed there and then to help Jo. She would walk again without all that tackle. He knew that was her main ambition, and now, it was his.

Over the next few months, he had been happy enough, but Jo had become very quiet and still did not seem happy. He thought it was because she was tired. Mam was always giving her jobs to do, like getting breakfast for him and Harry, who had become very moody and would not help them, and Mam didn't ask him to do anything. After eating, Jo had to sweep the kitchen floor, not easy for her. If Mam was out of the way, he would do it for her. He had only done it once when she was nearby and had got a clout round the head, as did Jo, and Mam had shouted at her telling her she had told her to do it herself.

From before the twins had been born, Jim had started doing Jo's exercises which was why Jo said he spent a lot of time in her room.

He got off the bed carefully so as not to wake his dad. He sat in the chair that was in the bay window. He looked out over the rooftops and went back to his thoughts.

He had been so jealous of the extra attention Jim had been giving her, although it was more that he wanted to spend time with her himself.

Jo had been so busy especially after the twins arrived. That was when he had first tried to get friendlier with Harry, and he would lie in bed trying to talk to him, only to be grumpily told to shut up.

After Mam had gone back to work in the pub at night, Jim had spent even more time with Jo.

He remembered one night Jim had gone to the pub and he had gone into Jo's room, only to find her crying her eyes out.

He had asked her if the exercises hurt that much and that she should tell Jim to be careful.

She had shouted at him to get out and leave her alone. He had tried to say he only wanted to help, but she would have none of it, although she had eventually relented and said if you want to help run me a bath.

He had done that for her, and from then on, he knew the secrets and lies had started although he didn't know why or what, but he meant to find out.

He always knew Mam had little time for him and Jo, but it had become his normal, and you can get accustomed to anything in time.

He spent a lot of time at Nanna Mary's. He loved going there. She was so funny. She had loads of funny ideas. He remembered her coming home from the market with those brown paper carrier bags with string handles, that she would carefully fold to use again, full of new clothes.

He would ask her who they were for, and she would reply, 'Whoever they fit.'

She had a long sideboard, that she was very proud to call a G plan, under the sitting room window. And under it was loads of shoes. He remembered Jo asking her whose a particular pair was, and she said, 'Whoever gets up first,' and they would all laugh at her. In her house, 'first up best dressed' definitely applied.

One night when her Harold had asked him if he wanted to sleepover, he had been thrilled, and when they had gone into her sitting room, she had been sitting in her underskirt on the settee with her feet in a bowl of water.

'Come in, lad, sit you down. I'm just washing my feet before I get in the bath.' He had been mystified, why anyone would do that.

When she had gone into the bathroom, he asked Alice why she did that. She said she didn't know, but she always did it. They had all had a good laugh that didn't affect the love they felt for their mam and Nanna.

He went back to thinking about Jo and Jim. They appeared to have become very close, but the strange thing was it was only when Mam was out. When she was around, they hardly spoke. Alarm bells started ringing, but he didn't want to go there.

In 1957, when Johnny had arrived, Jo had a funny illness that had taken thick end of a month to get better; he remembered telling his mam that the head teacher had been asking him about Jo.

'You keep your mouth shut,' she had shouted at him. 'if I ever hear you have been talking about any of us, it will be the last thing you ever do, and do you hear me?'

It was about that time he and Jo had gone on a holiday with Dad, and he had made the very hard decision to stay there. It had been the hardest thing he had ever done, but for once, he had thought about himself, and he knew he had to make the break. He wasn't surprised when Mam had agreed so easily.

He had kept in touch with Jo, and she had holidayed there again, and all in all, he had a good life.

His mind flashed back to the one and only time he had come back to visit Mam and the family.

He had woken about midnight and set off downstairs to get a drink of water. He remembered how different the house sounded at night; he could hear the little sleepy noises the babies made.

The street lights cast shadows through the landing window. He had stopped on the landing halfway up the stairs. He liked the flocked paper Jim had put up. He could still smell the paint even though it had been done over a week ago.

He stopped in his tracks. He hadn't realised anyone was up, but he could hear voices. He daren't move. He was afraid his mam would find him there, if he went back. One of the stairs creaked, so he stayed very still. Many times over the years, he wished he had gone back no matter what.

Jim was very angry as he shouted, 'What's wrong with you? Are you stupid? The school has told you the things he is up to, twagging, pinching things. When he is there, he is bullying the younger ones and taking their treats and dinner money, and you say he is a good boy.'

'You never understand our Harry. It's taking him time to adjust to not being the youngest. He is looking for attention, that's all.' Mam sounded as if she was crying.

'What a load of rubbish with all the kids in this house! He should be used to it by now. You always make excuses for him.'

There was a crash; he knew Mam had thrown something, probably a mug, at Jim.

'Why shouldn't I? You're fussing over Pete being here. Well, you can stop now. He is not yours. You only have to look at him and his precious sister to see they are both Sam's. I have told you this before, but you don't listen.'

'I only have your word for that. How do I know Harry and the rest are mine? You always did like to put it about a bit.'

'You bastard, how can you say that? You know they are all yours, and in any case at least I look at men, not little girls.'

There had been a loud slap, and he had been very shocked as this must mean Jim had obviously hit his mam.

'You bitch, it's a pity you aren't more like Jo. She will be twice the woman you could ever be.'

He had pushed a chair out of the way so hard it had hit the door that led into the hall.

'I swear if you ever hit me again I will have you locked up, and then I will put that little bitch away, the way you are all trying to do to our Harry.'

'You have no need to worry about that. It will be a cold day in hell before I ever touch you again in any way at all.'

He heard Jim go into the kitchen and knew he would be coming upstairs, so he strode over the stair that creaked and went back into the bedroom he shared with the boys.

He had known they would stop arguing now. They never did it where they thought the kids could hear them. He was very upset to think what he had been told about who was whose father in the past had been true. All these years he had tried to convince himself it was just Mam trying to hurt them.

What had they meant about throwing it around? *And* our Jo, what is 'it'? Why should Jim go to prison and the police be involved? He couldn't understand it. With hindsight, if he was honest, some horrible disgusting thoughts had tried to penetrate his mind, but he had blocked them out.

He had thought about it most of the night, just dozing for a few minutes here and there. He still hadn't come up with any reasons; he would later, much later.

Chapter Twenty-seven

It was quite soon after that night that Harry had been taken away. Mam had been inconsolable, and it was a good job Jo was there, or the others would have not been looked after.

One day when he had travelled up to see Nanna Mary, he slipped away and went to see Harry. They refused to let him in to start with, but he persisted telling them he had come from Wales. Eventually, they relented.

He was shown into the visitor's room and told to wait there while they fetched Harry.

The building was very imposing. The sort you visited with school, like a stately home type of place.

The walls were very large, and you could tell by the windows, they were very thick. It had turrets on all four corners, and ugly little gargoyles at intervals around the outside.

The only thing that spoilt it was the bars at the windows, which had beautiful leaded patterns on them.

He was trying to imagine who might have lived there originally when Harry came in.

'Hiya, let's go outside,' he said as he went back out of the room.

They sat on the front step. The doors were enormous and looked as if they would be hard to push open, but they had some sort of spring thing helping with that.

'How are things?' he asked tentatively. He never knew how Harry would react.

'Oh, it's OK here when you get used to it. I am lucky. Only my room is small, but I am on my own, and I love it. How're things at home?'

'All right, but Mam still cries a lot over you. Jo is still looking after the little ones, and Jim is still just the same.'

'I don't care about her crying. She asks for it. I will promise you one thing. I will never go back to live in that house. They are keeping me here until I am sixteen. Then I'm joining the merchant navy. My social worker is helping me with it.'

'But I don't understand why, Harry, Mam dotes on you. Is it because of your dad? You do know Jim's your dad, don't you?'

'Oh, so you do know Jim is my dad, not Sam.'

'Yes, I overheard an argument a few weeks ago, and Mam threw it at Jim. Although, to be honest, she had told me and Jo when we came home from Wales, but me being me tried to hide my head in the sand.'

'Sorry you found out like that. She had been telling me for years, from being quite little. She said I had a new Dad. She thought I would be impressed.'

'Being in here seems to be good for you.' Pete was surprised at the change in Harry.

'Yes, it is great, and they are arranging for me to go to Trinity House at fifteen, then joining the merchant navy as a cabin boy at sixteen.'

Harry's face lit up while he was telling Pete his plans and the help he was getting.

'If I like it, then my social worker will help me join the Royal Navy, and on top of that Nanna Mary has said I can live with her when I am on leave. So how's that for a future?'

'I am so pleased things are coming good for you. Harry, can I ask you something? During the argument I overheard, Mam kept referring to throwing it about and our Jo. Do you know what she meant?'

Harry jumped up and headed off up the big stone steps to the house.

'How the hell should I know? I have had enough today. Let me say it's a pity for our Jo she isn't in here. She would be better off.'

Pete grabbed his arm. He was the stronger of the two, and Harry stopped in his tracks.

'What's going on? Why would she be better off in here? Harry, tell me what's going on.'

'Look, Pete, it's not my secret to tell. Ask our Jo yourself. I am sorry. Please believe me.'

Harry was just as upset as Pete, and he could see that.

'I will ask our Jo. Can I come and see you when I am visiting again? And maybe we could write to each other.'

'Yes, that would be good. You first though, then I will have your address written down. Look, I have to go in. They don't like us out for too long, and we have been here over an hour.'

Pete was shocked by Harry coming over and hugging him.

'It's good having a brother again.' He smiled. 'Even if it is only half of one.' He turned up the steps laughing and stopped at the door, waved, and went inside.

Pete had a lot to think about now; he knew Jo wouldn't tell him anything. So he was no nearer to knowing the truth.

Chapter Twenty-eight

A month after his visit with Harry, Pete had come to Nanna Mary's to go on holiday to Cumbria with her and two of her boys, the second set of twins Bruce and Howard. They were five years older than him, but they had always got on very well, so he was really looking forward to this holiday.

Nanna Mary was originally from Appleby and liked to go back when she could, to visit her family.

On the train journey, she had been telling them some of her memories.

'Eh, we had some great times when I was a bairn. Appleby is right at the foot of the Pennines, you know. And that is a sight to behold any time of the year. It will be beautiful now in June, and as a real treat I will take you all to the famous horse fair. That's if your good, mind.'

They had all laughed, as they knew 'wild horses' couldn't have kept her away.

'Our house is just at the back of borough gate. Our family have lived there for over seventy-nine years. My brother stayed in it when my parents died, and he gave the rest of us some money to make up, but we are quite happy to keep it in the family.'

Mary had continued without expecting any comments from any of them.

'Yes, it's on the main street. There are some real posh houses along there. Some of them are even Jacobean. You know what that means, don't you? They should have told you about that at school. Well, ours is Victorian, and right there in the middle of the road is Moot Hall, and would you believe that goes back to the sixteenth century!'

Bruce interrupted her, 'What's a Mott hall, Mam?'

'You silly hapeth, it's not a Mott hall. It is a Moot Hall, and that's what that school of yours should have taught you. What do you do there?'

'Mam, me and Howard left school two years ago.'

'Well, how am I supposed to remember these things? Anyway a Moot is another name for a town, so it is a Town Hall. What are youse two doing if you aren't at school?'

'Eh, Mam, we work on the docks with our dad.' Howard was laughing his mam never got any better. But with all the kids she had, who could blame her.

'Here we are pulling into the station. Look quick up there. Can you see the big Norman Castle up there on the hill, look? In there is a trust which works to look after rare breeds of farm animals, things like pigs, sheep, and the like, as well as birds like waterfowl, pheasants, and all types of poultry. If I remember right, I think they also have owls and eagles and the like. Won't that be just grand for the three of you?' It was a statement more than a question.

As they walked to their 'hotel', that's what Mary called her brother's house where they would be staying, she remembered something else.

'Do you know there is a really famous school in Appleby, one that that the president of America—oh what's his name?—anyway, his two older brothers went there. I've got it—George Washington. That's who it was. He was supposed to come here as well, but his dad died so he had to stay in America.'

Mary stopped and folded her arms emphasising how proud she was for being able to tell them these things. She was very proud of where she was born.

Uncle Stan showed them to their room. They had to share, but they thought it was great. The twins had a double bed, and Pete, a single.

During the day, she took them to see the sights. Stan stayed home because his walking was not so good. He was seventy-five and the lads thought that to be ancient!

The high spot of the week was when they went to the horse fair; this had moved to here in the nineteenth century. Prior to that it had been in Howden in Yorkshire. It was known to have the highest concentration of horses for sale than anywhere in England, a boast now belonging to Appleby.

It was a balmy June morning that would be a very hot day; they were watching the gypsy lads playing with their horses in the sparkling water of the river. This was also how they washed them to get them ready for selling.

Mary was looking at their faces and said, 'It's got to you all, hasn't it?'

'What's got to us, Mam?' asked Howard, and the other two looked at her.

'The ancient ones weaving their spells, that's what. It's the magic of the horse fair. It gets to everyone who comes here. Just look at the faces of the people watching.' She pointed around her at the sightseers who were standing on the bridge with them.

They looked at the people, who were mesmerised watching the beautiful horses and ponies—piebald, skewbald, palominos, and many others—being washed and groomed in the River Eden.

They were being made ready for sale.

'It's folk like them that's spoiled it for others,' Nanna had grumbled, while staring at the television crews filming the horses, gypsies, farmers, dealers, and spectators who were just here for the day.

'All them lights, cables, and cameras get in the way. They should be stopped.'

Mary appeared to be deep in thought.

'Well, I suppose in a way it's good that they can take this wonderful sight into the homes of the poor folk who can't be here,' she said.

They had walked around the gypsy caravans. Pete thought he had never seen anything so wonderful, with their bright colours painted on them. Some of them were horse drawn and some had engines. There was at least one dog lying by each caravan and bright-coloured washing hanging on ropes tied to the trees, or laid on the hedges to dry in the summer sunshine. It seemed everything was sleepily basking in the sun, which also demonstrated the wonderful variety of colours.

What a wonderful day and fantastic holiday they had! But all too soon it was over, and they had to return home.

Chapter Twenty-nine

Pete had been to see Harry before he got the train back home. He had landed a really good job as a solicitor's clerk and was studying on day release at the college. He wanted to go into law, but he knew it would be a long hard slog to achieve it.

He had also come out and told them who needed to know that he was gay. He was seeing a really nice guy called Steve, but he wanted to take it slowly as he had so much going on in his life.

Most people took his news very well and didn't really care as long as he was happy. However, his mam had said it was his dad's influence. He wasn't bothered what she thought. He had expected it.

He had called at Mam's before he caught the train.

'Hi there, how are you all?' he called out as he went into the kitchen.

Pat had jumped off her chair and ran into the hallway crying.

'What's wrong? Why is Pat so upset?'

'Our Jo has vanished. She was up and gone when we got up this morning, and we have no idea where she's gone.'

'She will be at Nanna's. You know she often goes there.'

'Not this time. Our Lynne has been to ask my mam, but she hasn't seen her. Now she is worried as well. That little bitch! She doesn't care who she hurts.'

Val was livid; she was trying hard not to let it all out as she had Luke on her knee.

'She is an ungrateful bitch. She has taken most of her things, even that bloody eiderdown off her bed, and how the hell she got that in a bag I'll never know.'

'Have you phoned the police?'

'We tried, lad,' Jim said. 'They don't want to know she is sixteen and a runaway. That means she is old enough to leave home, and cos she has taken her stuff, she knew what she was doing.'

"Course she did. Now look how upset the bairns are, and that's your precious sister, she is supposed to care about them.' Val was still showing her anger.

Pete was not buying any of this.

'Hold on here. Jo would not leave Nanna or the bairns without good reason. What's going on here? There have been secrets for years here, and it's got worse since she had that baby. Now tell me the truth.'

His mam told Lynne to take the others out to play, all except Pat, who was still in her bedroom crying.

'You sit down. We have some talking to do.' Val pushed a stool towards Pete. Even at fourteen, he looked and acted like a man.

He sat down very reluctantly; he knew he wasn't going to like this.

'Right now, let's get some things straight. I do not want shouting around our Luke. He can't handle it.'

Her voice was very quiet, and it was obvious she was trying to hold her temper.

'We have been to the police, both Nannas, our Madge's, and our Jeans. We have phoned your dad and checked with the few friends she has. The police said what Jim told you. She is now classed as a runaway, and there isn't much they can do. As for the father of her kid, he knows no more than anyone else.'

'Tell me who he is. He'll tell me everything when I have finished with him.'

Pete was also finding it very hard to control his temper.

'Look, if Jo had wanted you to know who he is, she would have told you last night while I was at work. She and Jim had a row about babysitting. He ended up slapping her and sending her to her room. That's the last we saw of her. Like I said, she is an ungrateful little bitch, after all we have done for her.'

Pete got up and headed for the door. He turned to look at Val and Jim.

'She is not ungrateful or a bitch. There is more to this than you are telling. And one day I will find out the truth. She would never go without a better reason than that, and you are sure gonna miss her. You will have to look after your kids for a change. Our Harry's right. He is in a better place.'

Val jumped up.

'When have you seen Harry? They won't let him have visitors. I know cos I have asked repeatedly.'

'No, they will let him see anyone but you. He has told them he never wants to see you again.'

Pete was somehow taking comfort from seeing his mother cry.

'That's a lie, course he wants to see me, I'm his mam and I love him.'

'Oh yes, we all know how much you love him. I used to be jealous but not anymore. I don't want your love, nor do the others, if you love them the way you have our Harry.'

Jim put his arm round Val, and trying to help he said, 'Look, love, he will be sixteen before you know it, and then he will be coming home. So don't let this one upset you anymore.' He had nodded in Peter's direction.

'Oh, didn't you know? When he is sixteen, he is joining the Navy. He is going to Trinity House first, and then going to sea. Oh, and if you were wondering, when he is on leave, he is gonna stay with Nanna Mary. He will not come near you.'

He opened the door and left them sitting there. All he could think was what a good job he had left when he did, and wherever Jo was he hoped she would be safe and happy. There was nothing he could do until she contacted him.

Chapter Thirty

Pete had gone back to Wales and kept in touch with his nannas and Harry; letters from and to Jo were exchanged through Nanna. Eventually, Jo's friend had got in touch with him, and now this.

He could hear someone saying his name. He struggled and opened his eyes, and he could see someone in a white coat.

'What's happening? Where's my dad? How did I end up here?'

'Hello, I'm a doctor. You are in the casualty department at Scunthorpe Hospital. Your dad is here, and you passed out and fell off the seat in your hotel room.'

'Passed out? Don't be daft. I don't pass out.'

'I know this is strange, but you did pass out, and your dad rang for an ambulance because he couldn't wake you.'

'Well, what's wrong with me then?'

'We are running some tests, but as I understand it, you have had a rough time and are very worried about your sister, who is a patient here. All of that could be what's caused this.'

Pete felt his head where it hurt most, and found a dressing on it.

'What's this?'

'We had to put some stitches in a cut, but it's going to heal. No problem. And I have checked upstairs. Your sister is improving all the time. They say she is over the worst, so try not to worry too much, or you will be no good to her or anyone else.'

Pete soon recovered. He thought it was more due to the fact Jo was coming on in leaps and bounds, than anything else.

Harry came back to see them both a couple of times, and Pete decided he would have to share something else with him to help him make something of it.

Chapter Thirty-one

He had arranged to meet him on the pier at Hull. Easy for them both to get to, as Pete was staying in a B&B in Scunthorpe each weekend when he came from Wales to visit Jo.

They were sitting in the cafe on the Pier. Harry looked very smart in his uniform. He loved his life, which was obvious to anyone, in the way he looked, his body language, and he walked tall and proud.

'Right, Pete, come on, what's all the mystery? Why all this cloak-and-dagger stuff?'

'I want you to read this. Jo sent it to me two years ago, and I have been worrying about it ever since. She even asked me to move back to Mam's, which I couldn't do, but the fact she asked means something serious was going on. Read it and see what you think.'

Harry took the letter from him and started reading.

My dearest Pete,

I have missed you so much over the last few years, and I know you would be upset at me not getting in touch after I left Mam's 6 years ago. Is it only 6 years? So much has happened, it seems a lot longer.

I have been writing to Nanna for a long time, as you may be aware, but I swore her to secrecy about where I have been.

I needed to sort myself out before I could get in touch with you, as I knew you would not stop until you found me.

I am still married with 3 beautiful children. Gail is now 4—Ben, 3, and little Tony is the baby of the family. Ben and Tony are like us with their colouring, and everyone says they are like me. But you never see it yourself do you? Gail is blonde which could be from Mam or my husband, Roy, who is also blond.

He is very good with them, especially Gail but girls are always close to their daddy. So people tell me, I wouldn't know.

I have come to the conclusion you have to make the best of what you have. There is no such thing as paradise in this life.

Please don't try to find me, Pete. I have a friend who is a long distance lorry driver, and he posts all my letters for me, from different parts of the country so the post mark won't help you.

I know it will upset you that you can't visit us, but give me time, Pete. That's all I need—time.

I have also been writing to our Pat, and that's why I have written this letter. I am really worried about her, and I don't know who to turn to for help. I did think about our Malc, but he is only 19 and I can't be sure how he would react.

I send the letters to Lilly round the corner from Mam, and she has been really good not telling our mam. I do not want her to know where I am. We have moved from the caravan where you last saw me, and we now have a council house, but that's all I am telling you for now.

Pete, I have written this for 2 reasons—one to let you know I am all right, and the other to ask you a massive favour.

I am worried stiff about our Pat. You know she isn't too bright with her hearing problems and her letters are hard to decipher, and before you start thinking, she gives the envelope to Lily who addresses it. Pete, I can't say there is definitely something wrong. It is just a hunch, but it is enough to scare me rigid.

Harry stopped reading and looked at Pete. Neither spoke, but they were both very concerned. Harry's normal smiley face had gone.

I am sure she is in danger from Jim. I can't tell you what, only that she must not be left on her own with him. I am begging you, Pete, please don't say a word to Mam or Jim, or it will be our Pat mainly and me that will suffer.

I am going to ask you a massive favour. Could you move back home and live with them to protect our Pat? She can't protect herself. She is so gullible.

Please trust me, Pete. I would never have written this if I had any other choice. I will make it up to you. I will write more often, and if you want to write to me, send it to our nanna, and she will send it on. Remember there is a chance that I am wrong, so please don't say anything to our Pat, but I really need your help with this.

I love you very much.

Your loving sister

Joanna

PS: I talk to the bairns about you all the time, and it feels as if they know you.

Harry put the letter on the table and looked at Pete.

'Let's have another coffee, then we can talk.' He got up and went to the counter.

When he sat down again, they both sat for a minute, obviously gathering their thoughts.

'Right, is this why Pat moved in with Nanna Mary a couple of years back?'

'Yes, I could never go back there to live. I couldn't stand it, and I also have a life in Wales, and they would never accept Steve. So I did the next best thing by getting her out of the house.'

'My mind is working overtime. Do you think he was hurting the two of them in the way I do?'

Harry couldn't even say what he thought had been happening.

'Yes, Harry, I do. It makes me sick, but why would our Jo write this? You know she must have been frantic with worry to do that.'

Harry's face was very dark with anger, and it was obvious he was struggling with his thoughts.

The cafe was full as the ferry was due in any minute; this meant they were both struggling not to let others see they had a problem.

He stood up.

'Come on, we can't talk in here.'

'Hang on, Harry. The ferry is due any minute, and then this place will empty. And it is pouring down out there.'

'Bugger the rain. I can't sit any longer. I need to walk and clear my head.' He walked to the door and left.

Pete grabbed his duffel coat off the chair and ran after him.

He caught up with him near the warehouses that lined the streets near the pier.

'Come on, Harry. You know something, don't you? Just what has been going on? Come on, I have been kept in the dark long enough.'

Pete was almost running to keep up with him. He wasn't as fit as Harry now, and he was almost out of breath.

They passed the statue of King Billy, and neither of them looked for the stirrups.

When they reached the old church in the market place, Harry stopped and sat on the church wall.

'Now you've stopped galloping. Will you please tell me what's been going on? Why has that letter upset you like this? You insinuated something years ago when you were in the Marfleet Lane home. I put that down to you and our Jo not getting on. But it's more than that, and I want to know what.'

Pete was very angry. It got to him that Harry knew something he wasn't telling, and this time he would not let it go.

Harry was looking at him with complete shock on his face.

'I never hated her the way you think. Is that what you have always thought?'

'Never mind about what I thought. Tell me the truth. Please, Harry, please.'

'OK. I know how much you love our Jo and so do I. It is possible to love someone and still be jealous of them, and that is how I used to feel. Remember the night the twins were born, you and her cuddled up in your bed, giggling and talking, I felt so shut out and jealous. And that is how it stayed.'

Harry was walking round in circles as he talked; it was as if he couldn't keep still.

Pete got up and went to sit on an empty market stall with its canopy still in place.

'Come and sit here, Harry. At least it will keep some of the rain off. I am sorry I never realised how you felt, but we never meant to shut you out.'

Harry calmed down a little and sat down, but he couldn't look Pete in the eye.

'I was jealous, but it started very early on. Look, please don't interrupt me now. I need to say this, and I won't if you stop me.'

Pete reassured him he was all ears and would not interrupt. He now realised he was finally going to be told the truth.

Chapter Thirty-two

'I would have been about four or five, I aren't sure. Anyway it was when we moved onto that estate, and Jim moved in. Well, Mam had sat me on her knee. She was very excited, and thought I would be too. She told me Sam wasn't my dad, and that Jim was. I was very upset. I didn't want to be different to you two, and she thought I should be thrilled.'

He stopped to take a hankie out of his pocket to blow his nose. Pete knew he was close to tears, and he did as he promised and kept quiet.

'Mam had said Jim would look after me cos I was his son. Well, she couldn't have been more wrong. Within what seemed like no time at all, Jim started doing Jo's exercises and spending a lot of time with her. Well, one night I woke up for toilet, and as I passed Jo's room, I could hear him. I peeped through the crack where the door hadn't shut properly, and he was in there doing things that he had done to Mam. I had seen them when they thought I was asleep. Anyway that did it for me. At that time it just meant he cared for her more than me, and the jealousy got worse.'

'Are you telling me that from her being about eightish he was interfering with her, and you did nothing?'

'Pete; *listen* to me, will you? I was too young to know what was happening and too consumed by jealousy. I was in Marfleet Lane before I realised what he had been doing, and our Jo ran away not long after that. I didn't know what to do, but I do now.'

They both sat there in total silence for some time. The truth always hurts more than what you want to believe.

Firstly, they agreed at least Pat had been safe for the last two years and hoped he hadn't touched the other girls. They weren't disabled in any way like Jo and Pat had been. Maybe that had kept them safe.

The bone of contention was what should be done and who would do it.

Chapter Thirty-three

The telephone was ringing as Jim walked in the door from work.

'You can get that I have had three calls with no one on the other end.' Val was busy cooking the tea.

'Hello.'

'Meet me at St Georges dock at 6.00 p.m. tomorrow, and just in case you haven't realised, it's Harry.'

The phone went dead.

'Who was it?'

'Another silent one. They'll get fed up soon enough,' Jim replied. His mind was spinning with what had just happened. He hadn't seen or heard from Harry in years. Why now? What's happened? He knew enough to keep quiet about who it was. Val would read things wrongly and would insist on going with him.

He finished work at four thirty and walked across to the pub near the dock, and he was the first one in when the doors opened at five o'clock. He had drunk three double whiskeys before leaving the pub at just before six o'clock.

The only person he could see was a big built guy with his back to him standing near the dock wall.

When he turned, he couldn't believe it was Harry. How he had grown up into a man from the boy he last saw.

'You came then. I thought you would chicken out.'

'Why should I chicken out? I was curious and wanted to see you again, son.'

'I am not your son and never will be. Curious, are you? Well, so am I, curious about our Jo and Pat.'

The colour drained from Jim's face, and he seemed to lose his footing, maybe with shock or the whiskey or both. Anyway he managed to pull himself together.

'What do you mean?' His voice was shaky.

'Your reaction means you know full well what I mean. What about the other girls? Have you touched them as well, you slimy filthy pervert?'

'No, I haven't touched any of them.'

Jim was very afraid. He could almost feel the anger coming from Harry.

'Don't lie to me. I know you have with Jo and Pat, and I want you to admit it and tell me about the others, and no flannel. I will know if you're lying to me.'

Jim was in a real quandary trying to decide what to do; he was terrified of what was going to happen.

'OK, yes, with Jo and Pat. I have touched them where I shouldn't but none of the others. I promise you.'

Harry lost control and moved towards Jim, who tried to step backwards to get out of his way.

Harry kept coming. 'You're the father of Jo's baby, aren't you? Do you know what I would love to do to you?'

Jim lost his footing on the slippery wood around the dock side. He tried hard, waving his arms around, trying to regain his balance, but failed. He let out a horrible scream as he fell over the wooden sleepers and into the water.

Harry walked over and looked down. Jim was floating in the water, his anorak acting like a lifebuoy. Blood had run into the water. Harry thought it might be from his head but wasn't sure. He decided Jim had got his just desserts and turned and walked away without a backward glance. He never even considered calling for help. If Jim wasn't dead yet, he soon would be.

Chapter Thirty-four

Val was devastated when the police came to tell her Jim had had a fatal accident. She told the children who were upset, but realistically, the younger ones didn't understand what had happened.

Telling Mary and his brothers and sisters had been traumatic. And none of them could understand what he had been doing on the dock wall, and he usually had a pint on the way home but never had got drunk on whiskey. A lot of unanswered questions.

Nanna had let Jo know, and she was upset because all she felt was relief. Unbeknown to her, she agreed with Harry that Jim had got his just desserts. There was no way she could mourn for him.

Val attended the inquest with Mary and Jim's brother Brian. The coroner's verdict was 'accidental death'. Jim had fallen probably due to the amount of whiskey they found in his blood, combined with how slippery it would have been following all the heavy rainfall. Apparently, Jim must have hit his head on the dock wall, and this had broken his neck. He was dead before he hit the water, confirmed by the fact that he had no water in his lungs.

The best they could do was being thankful that he wouldn't have had to suffer and he had died quickly.

Mary was devastated this was the second son she had lost. Her oldest, Edward, had been killed in the last few weeks of the war. And she couldn't stop crying, 'your sons should bury you, not the other way round.'

Val was more worried about how she would manage without Jim's wages. A widow's pension didn't go far. She had board from Malcolm, Lynne, and Barbara, but that was changing. Malc was planning on having his own pub, so his money would stop. Lynne was going to university next year, thanks to Val's Uncle Syd, who was supporting her financially, and Babs only got a small wage as a cadet nurse. And she had another two years before Johnny left school. How would she manage?

Pete had asked Harry if he knew anything about Jim's accident, and Harry asked the same of Pete. Obviously, both denied it; more secrets never to be told.

Jo had stayed away. She was not a hypocrite, and in any case, she was still recovering slowly. The social workers and the police had persuaded her not to go back to Roy. She thought about Tony wanting to kill his dad and decided she couldn't expose them to anymore. Roy had gone to court while she was in hospital and had been awarded custody of the children. She knew it was better for them not to have parents fighting and arguing, and Roy would look after them. The social services and probation services were involved. He had been fined £35 and put on probation for two years for what he had done to her. Sergeant Browning had been very upset even though he knew this is what would happen; if she had 'been living over the brush', he would have gone to prison.

Pete and Harry were the only ones who knew where she lived, and they helped with letters to and from Nanna.

Chapter Thirty-five

The big surprise was when she got a letter from Nanna via Pete, and in it was a letter from Mam.

My dearest Joanna,

I know this will be something of a shock to you, but Jim's death has freed me to say what I feel.

I am hoping I can do what I should have done years ago and explain how things were for me.

I am not looking for forgiveness. I am not sure how that works in this case, but I am hoping you will at least understand.

Jim should never have done all those things to you, and I should have protected you. But should haves and would haves don't help. It is true what they say—hindsight has 20/20 vision.

I am well aware how badly your husband beat you, especially when he had had a drink. Well, it was the demon drink that made Jim do what he did. I even tried to stay awake all night to keep an eye on him, but I just couldn't, and the sleep would always take over.

You know how sorry he was after; he couldn't control himself when he had a drink.

He always said it was because you reminded him of a young me! I don't see how. You are so much like your dad.

What I am going to tell you will come as a shock, but I have to tell you. I'm sorry, but your nanna has also kept secrets for all of my life. Jo, your granddad, was not my dad. Your nanna had me when she was single, and you can imagine how big that was in 1924. Anyway my nanna said she would bring me up with her little ones. My mam was her oldest, and you know they had a big family. Well, the youngest 2 hadn't started school, so I grew up with them, until my mam met your granddad and they got married and had your aunties, Madge and Jean.

My 'dad' seemed to resent me. He treated me very different to his two, and I suppose I reminded him of my mam's mistakes.

He hit me for years, and when your dad came along, I married him to escape from it. Yes, I was pregnant with you, but that wasn't the only reason. I'm sure your dad knew I never loved him as I should, and I am to blame for things going wrong.

When I got to know Jim better, he had lived near us for years, but we never really spoke, until I met him one night when I was out with my friend Marie. Anyway I knew by the end of the night, I had real feelings for him. We were meant to be together. We did try to resist and failed. After I had Harry, things had to change. Both Sam and I knew he wasn't his.

I did and always will love Jim with all my heart. We can't help who we love, can we? And in any case, with all those kids to look after, I needed him, and that is why I took his side. I haven't worked out how we will manage without him, but apparently, I can get an allowance for looking after Luke. So that will help supplement my widow's pension, and we had a small insurance policy with the Prudential.

I loved you as well, Jo. You are my firstborn, but not in the way I loved Jim.

Now that you are all grown up with a family of your own, you may be able to understand a little.

I never wanted you to live the life you have and for you to wind up losing all of your children, but I am sure in time you will get them back. And I have contacted your auntie Sarah and asked her what she knows about your little girl's adoption. If you think I should not do that, then let me know, and I will leave it alone.

Thinking about things, did you marry Roy for the same reason as I did your dad? Were you pregnant?

If you need any help, please let me do that for you, Jo. Better late than never, eh.

If you want to come over for a few days, you are very welcome, and I promise I will not tell Roy where you are. He rings regularly, looking for you.

Please write back and tell me if you want to come. I will send you the money for the fare, although I don't know how far you have to travel. I would love to speak to you, so if you want to ring, you know the number. I am here most days but have to work at night. I now do 5 nights a week. The landlord, George, is very good. If I am stuck, he will let Luke go with me and sit upstairs to watch telly. He is a good boy. He never does anything he shouldn't. A bottle of pop and a bag of crisps, and he is happy. He is usually asleep when I finish, but he wakes up and walks home as good as gold.

Please get in touch, Jo.

I love you very much.

The letter had made a difference although she couldn't understand why Mam had thought she had been pregnant when she got married and why it was important. And her mam still would not see things as they really were. Jim didn't need a drink to do what he did. Jo had started writing to her mam, but she still would not give her address, or tell her things that really mattered. That sort of trust had to be earned. However, Pete acted as a go between, or Mam would leave her letters at Nanna Mary's, and Harry would deal with them when he was on leave.

Chapter Thirty-six

Jo was finding it so hard to live without her children. She would go to Scunthorpe on her day off and stand out of sight at the end of the street, hoping to catch a glimpse of them. Sometimes a friend she had made in the bedsit would go with her. Alison was the one person who she could talk to and who helped her get through each day. She was to become a lifelong friend and confidante, a friendship that lasted over thirty years until she was cruelly taken with a brain tumour at the very young age of fifty-two.

Pete would often travel up to Hull when Jo was there. He would stay at Nanna Mary's, but he, Jo, and Harry, when on leave, would have days out together.

Pete's trip to Appleby, and all he had learned up there, seemed to have awoken an interest in visiting old places and learning more about them.

A favourite place for them all was Beverley; it had two markets called Wednesday and Saturday, because those were when they were held. Beverley means 'beaver meadows', so named because of the old course of streams where the beavers once played.

Of course, there is the famous minster, and Pete had read a great deal about it. Work on it was started in 1220 after the tower of the old Norman church that once stood there collapsed. It took 200 years to complete, and many admirers believe it is the most beautiful non-cathedral church in England.

One day Pete had collected Luke from Mam's, and they all met at Beverley Minster. Luke was always asking questions by signing. He needed to know things, so Pete was ready to give him an account of the history of it.

'Let's start at the beginning, Luke. The minster was founded in the early part of the thirteenth century, partly as a shrine to St. John of Beverley, who had about 250 years before that built the church of St John the Evangelist,' he spoke and signed.

Jo really enjoyed walking around with her three brothers, listening to Pete and his tales, especially watching the beaming smile and interest on Luke's face.

As they walked through the town, Harry bought them all a delicious ice cream from the Padgett's van, and the man had put lots of hundreds and thousands on Luke's, which had thrilled him.

Harry had vanished for a few minutes and then turned up with a gift for Jo. It was an exquisite little brooch, in the form of forget-me-nots, set with tiny blue sapphires.

'Oh, Harry, it is fantastic. You shouldn't have. I will treasure it forever and think of you whenever I look at it. Why did you choose forget-me-nots?' she asked as she gave him a big hug and a kiss.

'It just caught my eye, and I thought of you.'

In a few years' time, she would realise the significance of forget-me-nots.

As they walked around the market, they were struck by the number of London accents they could hear from the market stalls.

'You should hear them, Luke. They have a funny accent.' Harry laughed as he signed to him.

'Can you understand what they're saying,' signed Luke, 'cos I can't?'

Pete was laughing with them.

'Do you know it is a long-standing tradition for Londoners to sell their stuff here? It goes back to the nineteenth century, so some of them still come to sell their goods here today.'

'I thought they looked old, our Pete. Do you remember any of them?' laughed Tommy.

Pete pretended to hit him, and they all laughed together.

It was a marvellous day, which they all enjoyed very much; Luke nearly drove everyone mad at home telling them all about it, almost day after day.

It was quite amazing how the whole family could join in the conversation and automatically use sign language.

Before they left Luke, he came over to Jo in the back seat of Pete's car, gave her a big hug, then stood back and touched his eye, his heart, and pointed at Jo.

'I love you too,' she said and signed back to him.

Jo and Harry went to the station together to catch their trains, Jo back to Doncaster, and Harry to Portsmouth. Pete had driven home to Wales after taking Luke home.

Harry hugged her and said she should hang in there. She would get through this.

Jo admitted she had been tempted to go back to Roy. She would ring him twice a week in the pub, to ask about the bairns, and he would be very nice to her, begging her to come back. She was having real problems trying to decide what the best thing to do was. She was missing her children so much, it was unbearable.

Harry told her that it was her decision to make and no one could tell her what to do, but if she thought about it, and 'yes' came to mind without any buts, then maybe she should. But if there were any buts, she shouldn't.

On the journey back to Doncaster, she thought about what he had said and wondered when her rebellious brother got so wise.

Chapter Thirty-seven

Jo had caught sight of the children now and then. It was a good job she had taught them a little sign language, and the 'I love you' was signed between them. She knew they would never tell Roy she had been there.

Roy had told her about his new job as a 'tea boy' on the site of a new steel works being built. She had laughed at him being a tea boy. He had told her it was the best-paying job he had ever had. He had an arrangement with the local butcher and news agent. He sold breakfasts, bacon sandwiches, and all that kind of thing, as well as cigarettes and newspapers, so the money, in his words, was rolling in. Yet again, he begged her to return. She did agree to go and visit them at Roy's. She was worried, but she also knew he was desperate, and therefore, she should be safe enough.

After spending a pleasant afternoon with Roy and the children, she prepared to leave. Roy sent the bairns into the garden to play and pleaded with her to come back. She told him she would have to think about it. Hearing her friend's taxi beep his horn, she walked out of the house. As she was going through the gate, she heard someone shouting. She turned to see the guy next door, who was a friend of Roy's, coming up the path with a rifle in his hands. It was a shotgun, but Jo didn't know that. 'I will sort her out once and for all, Roy. She won't bother you anymore.'

Roy shouted, 'No, Jack, put the gun down.' At the same time, Alan, the taxi driver, had jumped out of the car, grabbed Jo, and threw her onto the back seat. He jumped in and drove away very fast.

They contacted the police, who visited the neighbour who had a licence for the gun, which they said they were going to revoke, and the gun had been taken away. He had been given a warning, but as he hadn't actually fired the gun, this was all they could do.

Roy had told her when she rang him that he had asked for an exchange of house from the council, as he knew she would never go back to live in the house he had.

When she rang a few weeks later, he told her he would be moving to another estate, a new one called Westfield the following week, and he hoped this would make a difference

She went to see them all in their new home, it was a very nice three storey house and maybe this could make a difference

After a great deal of thought, she gave in and went back to him. The whole family were worried about this, but understood she had to be with her children, and they all prayed she would be safe this time.

For almost a year, things had been really good. She had taken a job at a working man's club in town. The Peterson family went in there a lot. Roy didn't, but as other members of his family did, he didn't touch her.

However, as normal, he eventually started to drift back into his old ways; only, the bruises were always on her body not her face. She wouldn't say a word to anyone as she was ashamed of having made the wrong decision.

One night at work, June, the other barmaid, noticed Jo flinched when they passed in a small doorway. June asked what was wrong. Jo said nothing. June was a very strong character, and she pushed Jo into the cellar, and unzipped the back of her dress.

'My god, are you crackers? What are you doing living with a man that does that to you?'

'What can I do? I have nowhere to go, and he will come after us if I did. He will never let us go, and I can't go without the bairns. I have been there, and I couldn't stand it again.'

'You need a fella to look after you.'

'You have got to be joking. I never want another man in my life. Don't you think I have enough bother with the ones I have?'

'Listen to me. You have been used long enough so use them. Look, it's our break in ten minutes. We'll talk then.'

June zipped up her dress carefully, and they went back into the bar. Fortunately, it was quiet, and they hadn't been missed.

On their half-hour break, June told Jo that Ron, one of the taxi drivers that the club paid to take them home, fancied her.

'Well, I certainly don't fancy him or anyone else for that matter.'

'Look, he is a nice guy, and he would look after you and the bairns. Just show him you're interested, and you're home and dry.'

'I couldn't do that. How could I use him if he is a nice guy?'

'Think about it, Jo. You have lived with Roy all these years, and you don't love him. So what's the difference other than being looked after instead of bashed?'

They had gone back to work, but Jo's mind was elsewhere.

When they had dropped June off that night, Ron had smiled at Jo who was sitting in the passenger seat. She smiled back at him.

That seemed to open the door, and within a week, they would stop for a cuddle in the car before he dropped her off.

Within four weeks, they were having an affair, and Jo was amazed that she had developed feelings for him.

They made plans for the future. They would move town, and he could get a job in three different areas. He said taxis, tyre fitting, or bus driving.

They had managed to find a flat in Hull and made plans to leave.

Chapter Thirty-eight

Ron collected her and the bairns on a Friday morning, and he had a trailer that carried their belongings. Jo had only packed their clothes and a few of their toys, not difficult as they didn't have much.

Things soon settled down for them. Ron got a job as a tyre fitter with a part-time job as a coach driver.

Roy was ringing everyone they knew to try and find her, which was Jo's main worry, as she was still frightened of what Roy would do if he found them. He would definitely take the kids, and she could not let them go.

No matter what happened, she would keep the children.

After three months, Jo was walking down Anlaby Road when she saw Roy walking towards her.

'Here you are! Did you really think you could hide from me?'

'Don't start anything, Roy, or I will scream. If you want to talk, we can go in this cafe and have a cup of tea.'

'OK, I'm not going to do anything. Yes, let's have a cuppa as we do need to talk.'

Once he had bought the tea, they sat down and discussed what was going to happen. Roy explained how he had walked the streets looking for her, and he had recognised some toys Gail had left on the dresser in their bedroom window; being a ground floor flat, he had seen them.

He was going to court for access as he recognised they wouldn't give him custody now Jo had a home for them; the last time she was in a bedsit.

Jo had no choice but to agree to let him see the bairns, and it was arranged for the next day. Roy was staying in a B&B. They went their separate ways, agreeing he would come at ten o'clock in the morning and take them until three o'clock.

Ron agreed that she had done the best thing, and he agreed she should follow them the next day; he couldn't as he had a bus tour to do.

Jo had followed them, and they went around the shops over monument bridge. They then went down Whitefriargate to Woolworth's. Jo couldn't believe what he was doing. He must have told them to get whatever they wanted. They were having difficulty carrying the things they had chosen. She went over to him to let him know she was there and had seen what he was doing.

'Roy, you can't do that. You're trying to buy them. You're gonna make me out to be the bad guy if I say no now, but they should not be buying everything they see. It's not right. You are trying to buy them like you do the blokes in the pub, and I can't afford to do the same.'

Jo was nearly in tears with frustration.

The children came running over with their arms full, and Roy said, 'What have you got there?! This is too much. Let's look again. You can choose three things each, and then put the others back.'

They didn't argue and did what he had said.

'You're right, Jo. Now what do we do from here? Are you gonna come home with me? Or do we go to court?'

'You can do what you want, but I'm not coming back with you ever again. We're finished. I have had enough.'

'I can control it, you know. It was getting better. Was all those years so bad, that we have to end?'

'Not that bad, Roy. Think back carefully and remember not just the way you treated me but also the babies you kicked out of me. How our Tony nearly died as a result of you beating me and pushing me down the stairs. Then you didn't even come to see us, even though you had messages from the hospital telling you how very ill we both were. Tony was christened in the hospital! Did you know that? He was so ill! We are over!' She knew there was no going back now whatever happened.

The children wanted to see the ferry so they walked Roy to catch it. As they waved him off, Jo noticed she had forgotten she was still wearing his wedding ring; she took it off her finger and threw it into the River Humber.

She couldn't help but laugh as Tony said, 'Is that so the fish can get married, Mummy?'

Jo took the children and walked away. She had been too angry to discuss things with him today; however, she had agreed to ring him the following night in the pub.

Things settled down quite quickly, and for about six weeks, it seemed as if life would be good. However, she wasn't sure that Ron was completely settled. She thought maybe he was missing Scunthorpe and his old life.

On the Friday night she was at work in the bar of the local pub, she did think it very strange that he hadn't come for a drink and to walk her home. The couple in the upstairs flat would listen for the children. It was a bit scary walking through the estate and down Anlaby Road on her own. She ran in the door and stood resting against it; she had been really scared.

It was very quiet in the flat. She looked round, and Ron wasn't there. Eventually, she noticed a note on the bedside cabinet. She opened it with a feeling of dread.

Dear Jo,

Please forgive me, but I can't stay here. I miss Scunthorpe. I didn't tell you I have 4 sons by my first marriage, and I am about to be arrested for non-payment of maintenance. I will be sent to prison for this. I have tried to prevent this by using every penny I could, which also means I have not paid the rent since we moved in, and I am really sorry about this, but we have to be out of the flat by a week on Monday. Maybe your family will help you, Jo, but I can't. You will also hear on the grapevine that I have been seeing my old girlfriend Jean; she has met me when I have been driving bus trips. Anyway we are getting back together, and hopefully, the court won't find me.

I am sorry, and I didn't leave the kids on their own. I stood across the road in a doorway until I was sure you were home safe.

Don't bother looking. I will be long gone by now.

I am very sorry, Jo, and I hope you will all be all right.

Ron

Chapter Thirty-nine

Jo had contacted the estate agents on the Monday morning. She had been reeling all weekend trying to work out what to do. She didn't really blame Ron. She had used him, but she had grown to love him as well.

She couldn't dwell on that. She had to think about what she was going to do now. What would happen if Roy realised she was on her own. Where could she go if they got evicted? All these things had been going around in her head all weekend.

The estate agents had said there was nothing they could do. The arrears were too big for her to pay. Even if she could, with children of both sexes, they should not be sharing. Therefore, she needed to be in a three-bedroom place. The eviction would go ahead as planned

The council told her she could have a house as soon as she was divorced, but not until then as her husband was in a council house.

Money was very tight; Roy didn't have to give her anything from the house. He was supposed to pay her £13.50 a week, which he didn't. So she had signed it over to Social, and they paid her every week and would chase Roy for the money.

The NSPCC and social services told her there was little they could do; three-bedroom properties for rental were a lot more than she could afford.

The only thing they could offer her was a hostel on Harley Street, which was definitely not like its namesake in London. It was a very run down area with a high crime rate, and drugs were becoming a real problem. She would have to be in by 8.00 p.m. and out by 9.00 a.m., and they couldn't even guarantee they would get beds, and it would be very difficult to get beds together. That option was out of the question. She could not become one of the hundreds of homeless people, and even if she considered it for herself, she would never do that to the bairns.

Nanna didn't have the room, and in any case, her health was poor. So she wouldn't even ask her.

Mum had soon changed her mind about helping and said she had no room.

Desperation set in. On Tuesday night, she put the bairns to bed, asked the upstairs couple to listen out for them, and then got ready to go out.

She applied make-up in a way she had never done before, with black lines round her eyes, thick mascara, and a red lipstick she had bought in Woolworths. She turned the waist band of her skirt over and over until it was very short, and unbuttoned the top three buttons of her blouse.

Looking in the mirror, she thought, *There you are, Jo. You look like a prostitute. Now you can get money to help find us somewhere to live.*

When she got to the front door, she stood there trying to force herself to go through it. She was shaking like a leaf, tears pouring down her face bringing the mascara with them. She was terrified and couldn't do it. This made her feel even more of a failure. How could she help her bairns? She loved them so much. What was she going to do?

Roy came to collect them on the Saturday. Gail told him Ron had gone away, and he pushed his way through the door and headed for the kitchen to Jo.

'What are you going to do, Roy? Please don't hurt me. I have had enough this week.'

'I have no intention of hurting you. Look, why don't you come home with me. It won't take long to pack, and I will help you.'

For a fleeting moment, she thought about it but knew from previous experience she couldn't do that.

Tony had climbed on her knee just before he had left with Ron, and said, 'Don't you worry, Mummy. When I grow up, I will kill my daddy for making you cry and hurting you. Can I stay with you? I don't want to go with him!'

She had told him he must go, but they wouldn't be too long.

How could she expose them to being homeless, and Roy was very good with them all. It seemed as they got older, he seemed to be drawn more to the boys. The problem was when she was there, Roy would lose it.

When he brought the children back, they played in the bedroom while their parents talked.

She told him she appreciated him moving house and trying to make life better for them. But, she said, she was not going to make any hasty decisions, and asked if he would keep the bairns for a couple of weeks until she found somewhere to live.

He agreed and left with the bairns after they had packed their things. It was a very sad sight, watching them walk up Anlaby Road with all of their belongings in two black bin liners. Jo thought her heart would break. Would she be able to find another home for them? Would she lose them all over again? She wondered what she was going to do.

Chapter Forty

Jo had searched all over Hull, Beverley, Leeds, Bradford, Grimsby, and finally arrived back in Doncaster. She did this over a four-day period, stopping in cheap B&Bs and getting the same answers everywhere she went. The councils all said the same—as her husband had a council house, she couldn't have one until she was divorced. Three-bedroom properties were just too expensive for her to rent.

She had rung Roy every night. He had a phone in the house now, and she rang when she knew the bairns would be in bed. She just couldn't face trying to answer their questions.

Roy had started to get angry with her for being so stubborn; he had already been to his solicitor to go for custody.

All the things that had happened to her in her life were nothing compared to the thought of losing the bairns again.

She had a sort of cousin who lived in Doncaster, in a bedsit, the same one Alison lived in, and Jo got a room there.

Carol worked in Couplands bread and delicatessen. She told Jo they were looking for staff, and there was a vacant room in the house she lived in. She was worn out and decided she would go for the job and room. At least she would be earning, and she could save as much as possible.

The best thing that came out of her working and living in Doncaster was how the friendship had developed with Alison; she had a room on the top floor, while she was at a teacher training college.

Roy had become very frightening, and Jo had decided to change her name so he couldn't find her. It was very easy to do this. She took Pat as a Christian name, and Tony's full name was John Anthony, but she had always preferred Tony. So she added an S to the John and called herself Pat Johns.

About two months after she moved there, she came home from work to a card from the post office, saying they had a letter that needed signing for, in the name of Joanna Peterson. This filled her with dread.

During her coffee break the next day, she went to collect it. It had been forwarded from her solicitors. The words written in there were the biggest blow that she had ever been dealt.

Chapter Forty-one

At teatime, Carol came running up to her room, to find her in a dreadful state sobbing and crying and not making any sense at all. Carol checked she had taken the antidepressants the doctor had prescribed, made her a cup of tea, and managed to calm her down enough to find out what was wrong.

'We were so worried when you didn't come back to work after your coffee break. I told the manager you had a migraine, to cover. What's happened, Jo?'

Jo passed her the letter; Roy had gained custody of the children!

'How did he do that? Did you know about the court case?'

'Yes, I knew, but what could I do? They would never give me custody, living in one room and sharing a bathroom with six other people.'

Carol didn't know what to say or do, so she sat with Jo until she was falling asleep. Sneaking out of her room so as not to wake her, she bumped into Alison. After explaining what had happened, Alison agreed to listen out for her. Carol had arranged to go out later but would pop up and check on her before she went.

When she went up to Jo's room at 9.30 p.m., she had woken up, made a coffee, and was lying on her bed, apparently reading a book, although, if truth be known, Jo hadn't taken in any of it.

'Why don't you come out with me and Keith tonight? It might do you good.'

'No thanks, Carol. I have taken a sleeping pill and my other tablets, and I am going to lay and read until I fall asleep,'

'OK then. Alison is upstairs if you need her. I will see you later. Get a good sleep. That will help you think clearer.'

After she had gone, Jo lay with the book for about an hour. She thought to herself, *That sleeping pill isn't working. It does say one or two. I know I will take another one.*

Chapter Forty-two

When Jo woke up, she couldn't work out where she was. This looked like some sort of hospital.

'Now, there you are. You've woken up at last.' A very homely looking nurse walked into her room.

'Where am I? What happened?'

'Well, now you obviously have no memory of what happened. You see you took a full bottle of sleeping pills and a bottle of antidepressants. It's a good job your friend found you, or you might not have been here to tell the tale.'

'I didn't try to kill myself. I would never do that to my children. How long have I been here and where am I?' Jo was getting very distressed.

'Calm down, my love. You are in the psychiatric wing of Doncaster Hospital, and I never said you tried to kill yourself. Your friend explained what has been happening to you, and it has all become too much. It is very possible to do what you did, without realising what you are doing. Now get some rest, and the doctor will see you in a little while.'

Jo was so distressed to think she had wound up in a psychiatric hospital. She couldn't have taken an overdose. And how can you do that and not know?

Carol had visited her every day, and the hospital was classing her almost as next of kin. No one else seemed interested in her.

'How is she today?' Carol asked the charge nurse. 'She is worrying me.'

'She is a pretty poorly lady. She is shutting off from the world, refusing to speak, eat, or drink. The doctor is using hypnosis now to try and get her to open up. Once she is able to talk to us, she will improve, but if she refuses nutrition, we will have to give it to her another way. Anyway, let's see what happens with today's hypnosis.'

He led her into the viewing room where they could see and hear Jo.

'No, Jo, you are doing very well. You have told me a great deal about your marriage and your beautiful children. Now let's go back a bit and see what you can tell me about your life in Hull with your mam.'

Carol thought if she was in there, listening to the very calming and wonderful voice of the doctor, she would tell him anything.

Jo was now very tense and let out the most alarming scream; it made them all jump and look at her in total shock.

'No, Jim, no. Please, not again. Please, Jim, it hurts. Mammy said you are to massage my legs, Jim, not this. You can't touch me there. I will tell on you. Please, Jim, no, it hurts! Please no!'

She was crying so hard, talking was difficult.

'Jo, that's all right. Now listen to me. Now when I clap my hands, you will wake up and be ready to talk to me.' The doctor clapped his hands, and Jo woke up.

Over the next few days, Jo told the doctor everything that had happened to her from being a little girl until now.

She stayed in the hospital for another three weeks. The doctor was really good and very considerate. He was the first person she had discussed everything with from her childhood up. He helped her to see she had to make a new life for herself, and to understand the court would not swap custody around without good reason. It was unfair on the children who needed stability. In any event, without a home for them, she would not stand a chance.

He told her it was time to prove the people in her life wrong, show them she could make it without their help. Her mother, then her husband, had spent years telling her she would never amount to anything and couldn't get by without them. Now it was time to show them all.

They did discuss further counselling, but Jo said she couldn't talk to anyone else. And as Jim was dead, nothing would be gained from telling other people.

He did offer her medication, but only in small supplies if she felt she needed it. But she said no. She would sooner try without.

Her new resolve was harder in the silence of her room. Alison and Carol tried, but they were out all day, and the loneliness with only her thoughts for company was dragging her down. The shop had replaced her, and she now had to decide what sort of work she could apply for.

A week after her discharge there was a knock on her door. When she opened it, her dad and Pete stood there. Dad opened his arms, and she fell into them. He then passed a case to Pete and told him to pack everything. She was going home with them. For the first time in many years, she felt safe.

It turned out that the night she had been taken into hospital, Carol had given the police Roy's address as her next of kin. They had notified him, but he hadn't bothered telling anyone until Pete had visited to check on the children. He then went straight home and told his dad, and here they were. It was hard saying goodbye to Carol and Alison, but she knew whatever happened they would keep in touch, and Ali said she could come and stay whenever she wanted.

It took Jo about two months to recover enough to think of what she was going to do. She would never get used to being without her children, but she had to accept the courts would not change custody simply because she wanted them to. And in any case, she couldn't provide them with a home.

She had started proceedings for her divorce. Although when she rang or visited Roy and the children, he kept insisting she would come back to him at some point, and why she was dragging it out.

He had a housekeeper now who also had three kids, but the oldest didn't live at home. The younger two were with her, and Jo wondered how they all fit in a three-bedroom house.

One day, when she was spending some time with them, she asked Gail, who answered, 'Daddy said if anyone asked, I was to say, the girls are in one room, the boys in another, Jane has the third, and Daddy sleeps on the sofa. But he doesn't really. He sleeps with Jane.'

Jo was not at all upset by this. She just hoped he treated her better.

Chapter Forty-three

Jo had kept her appointment with the solicitors to start the divorce; she knew she had to get her life in order.

Mr Oxon was not how she had expected him to be. He was a jolly-looking person, slightly overweight and balding, nothing like she had expected a solicitor to be.

'Take a seat, my dear.' He held the chair for her and then took his seat in the enormous swivel chair behind his big mahogany desk. The office was warm and quite comforting with the warm-coloured desk. Even the chairs were maroon leather, and someone had thought about the layout of the room as even the austere filing cabinets had been put at the back of the room where clients couldn't see them.

'Now, my dear, can I call you Joanna? It sounds better.'

'Yes, but I prefer to be called Jo.' She was so relaxed. The big leather chair seemed to envelop her. 'All right, Jo it is, and my name is Charles. Now let's see what needs to be done. Did you write out the important things that have happened in your marriage?'

'Yes, I did.' She handed him the file she had brought with her. The secretary came in with a tray of tea.

'Oh my, I have a lot of reading to do here. It seems you have had an eventful marriage.'

'Writing it all down was so hard. It was like I was reliving it all. No one else will see that, will they?'

'Well, Jo, my assistant and secretary will see it, and the relevant points will be brought up in court. You are aware you will be questioned on everything you have put down, don't you? It is not going to be easy for you.'

'Yes, I am aware of that. I will just have to try, although I don't know how I will cope.'

'Don't worry too much just yet. There is a lot of work to do before then. I have already written to his workplace, asking for a breakdown of his last year's earnings, telling them if they don't send it, I will subpoena one of their wages clerks to attend the hearing. I have received this. Were you aware he has averaged £100 per week for the last year, and then he had the profits from his catering etc.'

'No, I had no idea. He never gave me anything. I worked very hard on farms during the day and behind a bar at night, just to pay the rent and feed us. I had to use Provident cheques and jumble sales to clothe the children.'

She was shocked she knew he had had money but not how much. 'We also have the police reports and medical reports. You are not going to have a problem getting your divorce. We have had the house watched since he has had the children. The NSPCC have been involved, but he has not left them once. If he had, they would have gone in and brought the children away,' Charles Oxon brought her up to date

Jo was amazed at this. She told Charles how Roy liked a drink and how she was sure he would go to the pub once the bairns were asleep. 'Well, his housekeeper looks after them during the day outside of school, and he stays in with them at night. We noted there are only three bedrooms, but as she came on the scene after you left, it has no bearing on the case. However, the lady whose details you gave us has stayed with her promise to you and says she will come to court if you need her to. She also asked me to tell you that she and her husband are back together, and he loves her son very much.'

'I am so pleased for her. She was taken in by Roy just the same as I was. How many lives has he hurt!'

Jo was now becoming upset; she sat upright on the edge of the chair. Charles came round and helped her up; even now she still had some pain in her chest from the injuries.

'Let's leave it there for now. I need to read through your file and try to understand how you have been living. The most important thing is for you to carry on trying to find somewhere to live. Your divorce is assured, but you will not get custody until you have a home for the children. Let's take one step at a time. I will see you again next week. My secretary will give you an appointment. The important thing is you hang in there. It will all come right eventually.'

Jo had spent a few days at her nanna's. In order to use a solicitor in Hull who was highly recommended, his office was in the Land of Green Ginger; *Isn't that an intriguing name for a street*, Jo thought as she walked down Whitefriargate. She walked very slowly onto Monument Bridge and then crossed over onto Queen's Gardens, where she sat on a bench. She remembered how these gardens used to be Queen's Dock, the first enclosed dock in the world, dating back to 1778; they used the world's first bucket chain dredger to clear away the silt. Jo thought how strange it was that in these circumstances she would remember another of Pete's pieces of information.

The tears ran down her cheeks. She had put some make-up on today and that was also running down her face. Jo neither knew nor cared.

Suddenly, she became aware of someone sitting next to her. The smell of body odour was the first thing she noticed. By her side was an old lady dressed in what could only be called rags. 'Eh, my dear, don't take on so. Whatever is upsetting you so much? It canna be that bad, can it? Talk to Meg and see if it will help.' Her voice was very soft and gentle, and Jo wanted to talk to someone so why not.

'I'm just saying goodbye to my old life before I look for a new one.' Jo laughed in spite of everything when she realised how dramatic that sounded.

'Don't fret so. Things are always darkest before the dawn. Eh, listen to me sounding all wise and brainy, which I'm not. Far from it, in fact.'

Meg shuffled in the seat, pulling the old black coat tighter and removing her headscarf. Her hair badly needed washing as did Meg. Her hair looked to be very long. It disappeared inside the back of her coat. It looked as if it was blonde but it was hard to judge. What did surprise Jo was Meg was much younger than she first thought; probably, no more than fifty. There was a hotdog stand on the corner; Jo thought she could do a good turn here.

'Would you look a hotdog and a warm drink, cos I would?'

'Eh, that'd be grand, if you're sure. I'm not begging, you know.'

Jo laughed and went to the stand and came back with two hotdogs, some packets of biscuits, and two cardboard mugs of tea. They ate in silence.

'Now that was grand. My name as I have said is Meg, short for Margaret. What's yours?'

'Mine's Jo, short for Joanna, but only my mam calls me that.'

'I know what you mean. I haven't been called Margaret in many a long day. Now why don't you tell me what the problem is? I may not be able to help, but it does help to talk.'

Jo explained about leaving Roy and what had happened with the children, how he would keep them as she couldn't give them a home.

'Right, now here goes. I think I can help a bit. The same thing happened to me in a sort of way. My husband was a fisherman. About twenty years ago, he drowned at sea. I was left with two boys, lovely boys they were. Philip and Charles we called them cos I love the Royals. Let me think. They will be about twenty-eight and twenty-six by now. Anyway, I couldn't cope. Losing my soul mate and dearest love destroyed our life. I took to the drink, and eventually, them there, social services, came and took me bairns away. That broke my heart, and I drank all the more until I lost everything. I have been on the streets about seventeen years now, although time becomes irrelevant.'

Jo put her hand on Meg's arm.

'Now, don't you stop me. I don't do this very often. The times may be wrong. The drink has puddled me brain, but the story's right. Anyway, losing my boys made me worse, and I drank more and more. I have no idea what happened to them cos I drank even more. I lost my home cos I didn't pay the rent. All me money went on booze. I took to thieving, shoplifting, and whoring just to buy booze. I ain't proud of what I've done, just the opposite in fact. But it's too late for me now. I can't remember when I slept in a bed my own, anyway. If I'm lucky enough to get a bed in a hostel, there is one on Harley Street, you know. That's good, but they are infested with bugs and the like. Sometimes someone in there might have a couple of pound, and they will give me it if I let them have their way with me. Don't look so shocked. This is what happens when you take the slippery slope I have taken. I eat what I can find in bins and on the streets. It's good late at night when there are lots of half-eaten fish and chips or Pizzas, and the like that people throw away, and some charity people come around with a soup kitchen.' She pulled a bottle out of her pocket. It smelt like turps to Jo.

'Aye, lass, this is meths. It's cheaper than booze. And anyway, unless I can buy the good stuff, booze ain't strong enough for me, and I cannot afford to buy that. Even if I could get into the shops, they usually tell me to get out cos I stink, which I knows I do. But there ain't no baths in the street.'

'I have a little money if it will help you.' Jo was feeling around in her pocket. 'I know about Harley Street. They told me about it when me and my bairns were losing our home.'

'Now, don't you do that, missy. You're gonna need every penny you can lay your hands on, and never take bairns into Harley Street. It's a nightmare for us old ones. Now listen to Meg. Don't you wind up like me and the hundreds of others living on the street. Don't look so shocked. I never would have though it could happen to me. What you have to do now is to think this is the start of a new life for you. It might be without your kids, and that'll always hurt, but you have to be the happiest you can. Then who knows what might happen in the future. Now you go and get on the train back to your dad's and then look at how you can show 'em all, even him up there.' She looked upwards and crossed her chest. 'Show 'em all you can make a new and happy life for yourself.'

As they walked to Paragon railway station, they were both thinking what a strange sight they must have looked to passers by.

'There, just in time. You've ten minutes before your train leaves. 'ave you got an 'ankie in your pocket?'

Jo pulled one out and gave it to Meg, who wet it at the nearby water fountain; she then cleaned Jo's face with it.

'There you go. Passable now. You get on that train, and you is wrong, you know. This is not ta-ra to your life but hello to your new life. And remember my words, keep yourself well and be a happy girl.'

Jo thanked her, shook her hand, and went through the ticket barrier towards her train. Meg pushed her way to the front and waved her off.

Jo would never forget the kindly lady who helped her today; as the train pulled away, she was deep in thought about where she would go from here. She hadn't a clue what was to happen, but she was going to try. She, however, had an important letter to write first.

Dear Mr Oxon,

Thank you for all the help you have given me, but I now know I cannot go through all that in court. It would crucify me to see my children with him, and to relive all the horrors again in front of all those people. I am moving away to try and put my life together. Once I have a new address I will let you have it. I know I do not have to ask this but please do not give it to anyone. If there is anything important you can send it to me. Is it possible for you to speak for me in court? If not then I cannot go ahead with the divorce.

Thank you again. I know this is cowardly, but I cannot do any other.

Yours sincerely

Joanna Peterson

Chapter Forty-four

Jo was reading through job adverts one day in the newspaper. She was having a coffee in a Scunthorpe Cafe while waiting to go and hopefully catch a glimpse of the bairns.

AUXILLARY NURSE REQUIRED AT GRIMSBY GENERAL HOSIPITAL. EXPERIENCE NOT ESSENTIAL AS TRAINING WILL BE GIVEN. ACCOMODATION AVAILABLE IF NEEDED.

Jo became very excited. This was as near her dream of being a nurse as possible. And Grimsby was near Scunthorpe, so seeing the bairns would be easier and she would have somewhere to live.

On the train back to Wales that night, she drafted her letter for the job, telling them she was waiting for her divorce but no more details.

Ten days later, she received her reply, offering her an interview, they also suggested that as she was virtually single, would she consider undertaking her enrolled nurse training, she was thrilled to be offered a date to go for the interview.

Jo was over the moon. Dad offered to lend her the train fare to make getting there and back easier, and Megan said she would pay for a room in a B&B the night before to save any rushing or panicking.

The interview went very well in the morning. Even though she was very nervous, and she had had to be honest regarding her medical history, the panel said that it would not be a problem if she signed agreements giving her permission for them to write to the psychiatrist and her GP.

She had a medical in the morning with no problems, and she was then given lunch prior to an entrance test in the afternoon. She was impressed with how she thought she had done in the test; the first part was the sort of things she had done with the bairns in their puzzle books—what number comes next and find the missing word etc. Then she had to write an essay on one of the following four subjects:

- The home you would like
- The wardrobe you would like
- A book you have read
- A film you have seen

Jo had no idea about homes, wardrobes, or films as money governed them. So she thought about books. She had just read one of Pete's called *To Sir With Love* that was made into a film, but she hadn't seen the film. So she wrote about this book as it covered a highly educated teacher who had to work in a rough town with the wildest kids, and how successfully he did that. The key issue was he was a highly educated teacher who happened to be originally from Jamaica. In the sixties, racism was not looked at the way it was later to become.

Two weeks later, she received a letter from the hospital, telling her she had passed the test demonstrating her higher than average IQ of 128. Therefore, if she wanted she could train for her state registration rather than enrolled. They had checked with her doctors who had verified she was safe to do this and said it would make a massive difference to her life.

Jo and her family in Wales were over the moon. She wrote to her nanna, to Harry, and her mam, and they were all pleased she was able to move forward. She was thrilled that her original ideas of what she could do were coming true. Mam thought she was crazy but agreed she had to give it a go.

Jo had also thought about travelling and even looked into joining Queen Alexander's Nursing corps. Following her talk with the recruitment officer, who had told her that in the event of her getting posted to a non-training hospital, her training could be suspended and take longer to achieve. However, if she qualified in civvies, she would automatically come in as an officer with much better pay and conditions. This was what Jo decided to do. Being posted overseas would maybe mean she couldn't see the children as often, but maybe this would help them settle into their new lives and her in hers.

Her last few weeks at her dad's was brilliant. She and Pete would go out and about on a weekend. They both enjoyed this precious time together. They would take Daniel with them most of the time.

North Wales is a beautiful place with the most amazing scenery; they rode on the Blaenau Ffestiniog mountain railway, which was a favourite of them all.

They also took a ride to a very special place as it has the longest name of anywhere in the world. None of them could say it, but the name is on the railway station and all over the area. Its full name is *Llanfairpwllgwyngyllgogerychwyrndrobwll—. . . llantysiliogogogoch,* which means 'the church of St Mary in the hollow of the white hazel near the rapid whirlpool and the church of St Tysilio near a red cave', although it is usually shortened to Llanfairpwll or Llanfair PG.

'Sounds more like directions than a place name.' Pete said, laughing.

No matter how they tried, they could not say it or even more remember it. However, it was good to see it after hearing about it over the years.

Chapter Forty-five

Her training started in January. She found it very hard in the beginning because it was all anatomy and physiology. She had discussed her fears with the principal tutor, who assured her she was doing all right. She might have to work harder at this stage but to stay with it because when she started on the wards, it would all become clearer and start to make sense.

'You are going to have to work hard for the next three years, but you will make it,' said Mr Lee.

'But it's so hard, and when we did the two days on the wards, one man died and another was very very ill. I went home and cried. It is so distressing.'

'Now listen to me. That means you have the makings of a very good nurse. Your intelligence is there. Your IQ proves it, and you have something these younger ones don't—you have experience of life and some of this will help you be much more understanding. Some of the practical things you will be doing we could train chimpanzees to do, but understanding and really caring comes from your own journey through life. You just have to remember that, and as for being upset, if you work as a nurse for the next forty years and ever meet a nurse who hasn't got upset over a patient, then they shouldn't be nursing. You have to care or you wouldn't do the job you have chosen. So go and enjoy your two weeks' holiday, then come back a new confident you. And remember, I'm always here if you want to talk. You're not staying in the Nurse's Home for the holiday, are you?'

'No, my brother is getting married in Portsmouth, and I'm a bridesmaid. Then I am going to my friend's. She did live in Doncaster but has now moved near Liverpool.'

'Right, you go and enjoy yourself, and I will see you in a fortnight.'

Jo had a brilliant time at Harry's wedding. The only family of Harry's there were Jo and Pete who was his best man, and Uncle Brian had brought both Nannas. Harry's wife, Lauren, was a lovely girl and obviously loved him very much. They had bought a house in Portsmouth with a view of the sea and invited Jo to stay whenever she wanted.

Jo then caught the train to stay with Alison who was now teaching at a school in Skelmersdale and loved it. They talked, laughed, and visited places. She made new friends through Ali.

They visited Knowsley Safari Park which was fabulous though scary; the big animals including the big cats were magnificent. However, the scariest was the chimps and monkeys. They sat on the car bonnet, roof, and boot, and played with the windscreen wipers. Alison was afraid they would break something that she couldn't afford to replace, but it was great fun and wonderful to see the huge variety of animals. They toured Liverpool, the updated Albert dock with all of the shops and museums. Then they went and found the statue of Eleanor Rigby, from the Beatles' song. It was hard to find as it isn't on a plinth or anything like that. Tommy Steel crafted a park bench with a lady in a coat and headscarf just sitting on it, and it is just sitting on a street; you could almost walk past it without noticing it.

She became good friends with Howard who was a teacher at the same school as Ali, and he lived with his partner Stuart. Jo was well at ease with gay people because of the time she had spent with Pete and his partner Steve.

The four of them had travelled all around Liverpool, visiting the cavern and seeing the Liver birds and the strawberry fields. The Beatles certainly had done a lot of Liverpool. They had another wonderful day at Knowsley Safari Park. It was fabulous seeing the animals close up in their own habitat.

They browsed through bric-a-brac shops in the small towns and villages in the area, and her last day there they spent at a local bird sanctuary in Burscough.

All too soon, the holiday was over, but she had had the best time ever. And she was quite happy to go home, as the Nurse's Home now felt to her.

Chapter Forty-six

Her room in the Nurse's Home was very small, but she had all she needed, except her children. However, Roy was very good at letting her see them. He even asked her to come in her uniform and see the bairns. She could also put them to bed. She found this more comfortable than she had thought. It was a relief to see him with another woman, maybe now she was free of him.

She had told Nanna, Pete, and Harry where she was.

Nanna had written every week, and she kept asking Jo to contact her mam, who had moved into her own pub with her new partner, Archie, but they had had to move to a place called Castleford in West Yorkshire. Jo was reluctant, however, with Mother's Day approaching. She decided to send her a card. A few days later, she received a letter from Lynne, inviting her to go to Mum's for a visit. As she had a weekend off, she decided to go, if only to see the other kids.

On the Friday night, Mum was very busy in the kitchen, so Jo helped out behind the bar. Generally, it was quite good, and she did enjoy her night, except for having to tell the regulars who she was. They knew she was related to Val as she had a look of her but had no idea Val had another daughter. She did feel a bit like a dirty secret.

She shared a room with Lynne, and that night, when they went to bed, she was amazed when Lynne said, 'That Les fancies you.'

'Who's Les? Don't be daft, and in any case I'm not interested in any men,' Jo replied.

'He's the tall, long, dark-haired one that talked to you whenever he could. He was drinking Pints of Bitter.'

Jo climbed into bed laughing and telling her she was imagining things.

The next day she was working the lunch time and the man Lynne had been talking about came in for a drink. It was very quiet, so they were talking quite a bit. Somehow they got onto motorbikes. After visiting Cadwell Park once with Roy, Jo had a secret yearning. She told Les what it was.

'I've always wanted to ride the chair on a motor bike racing outfit.'

'Well, that could be done. My mate Roy races with his brother. I could ask him to take you round the track if you like. Let me go and ring him.' He went to the phone box.

Jo was stumped trying to work out what to do now. Did she want to go out with this guy or any other guy for that matter? He did seem very nice though, and he was around her age. Maybe she should go. One date wouldn't hurt, and she might get to ride an outfit.

Les came back into the bar.

'Yes, Roy says he will take you with him when he can, and he has suggested we all go out tonight to talk about it. That would be us two and him and his wife, Jean. What do you think?'

'All right.' Jo wasn't sure, but seeing as it was a foursome, she thought she would be all right.

Mum wasn't happy but said nothing for a change. Jo knew from her manner something was wrong, but as she was going home the next day, she decided to keep quiet and make the best of the weekend.

They had a good night and all got on very well. She had no idea they were to become lifelong friends.

During the night, while Roy [it was strange how he was so different the other Roy didn't come into it] and Jean were playing pool, Les was talking to her about herself.

'Are you single?' he asked.

'Almost. I am waiting for my decree absolute to come through.'

'Oh, I'm sorry. Have you any children?'

Jo was amazed when she found herself telling him about the separation and what had happened with the children, even more so when he had said, if she wanted to talk he was there, but if she didn't that was good as well. Jo had never known a man who was so considerate, but she didn't know him well enough to tell him anymore. By the end of the night after they had gone back to Roy and Jean's with fish and chips, it was agreed that she wouldn't catch the train back to Grimsby. Les was taking her home. She was a little worried about what he would want in return but agreed anyway.

On the Sunday morning, her mum said they needed to talk, and over a coffee. It did strike Jo as strange that the others stayed out of the lounge.

'Jo, I know you were reluctant about me doing this, but I did it anyway. I wrote to Auntie Sarah about your baby, and she replied some time ago. But I didn't think you could deal with it, and your nanna agreed, but now I think you have turned your life around and maybe can deal with it now.'

'Mam, get on with it. What's wrong? What did you find out?'

'OK, I will tell you what happened. As you thought, your aunt knew who adopted her and kept in touch with them. There is very bad news, Jo. The baby died of a cot death when she was fourteen weeks old.'

Jo was in total shock, trying to absorb what was being said. Helen was dead, had been dead all these years. How did she not know what had happened? Why didn't she feel it? What should she do now? Mam put her arms round her, and Jo sobbed on her shoulder. After about five minutes, she sat up and pulled away from her mum.

'Why didn't you tell me? She was my daughter. I had a right to know. You have pulled some stunts, but I will never forgive you for this, letting me think my daughter was alive and happy, when she had been dead for years. Why didn't you tell me, and what gave you the right to decide what I should know?' The tears, anger, and grief all came out together.

'Jo, please believe me. I am very sorry. It took a while for your aunt to reply. She thought I would be too upset after Jim died to deal with it, and when she did write to me, I got in touch with Pete to see where you were. And he told me you had been in hospital and were having a hard time, so we decided to wait. It was me, Pete, and your nanna who decided this, not just me. Jo, I am so sorry.'

'What caused her to die? Was it because she was Jim's? Was she punished for what I had done?' Jo was rambling, trying to make sense of everything.

Val reassured her, and Lynne and Malc came in and helped, although they still didn't know the full story. The secret survived. Eventually, she calmed down and went for a bath. She needed time on her own to try and make sense of everything.

They had lunch at 3.00 p.m. when the pub closed for the afternoon, and at four thirty, Les came to take her home. Jo was obviously quiet on the journey home, and Les was the perfect gentleman. He dropped her off and set off back. It did go through Jo's mind that it was a four-hour return journey, and he hadn't even had a cup of tea, but when she got to her room all thoughts of him where gone as she lay on her bed and cried herself to sleep, thinking she had lost all four of her children. It was hard to put them all together as she had never known Helen, and therefore, her love was different to the other three.

Jo spent the next three weekends at Mum's pub, and despite her fears, she and Les did get closer, so much so that on her second weekend home, he had told her one day they would be married. He had laughed, and he knew she wasn't ready for that yet. After six months of trying to maintain a long-term relationship, Jo applied for and got a transfer to Pontefract General Infirmary, and lived in the Nurses Home there. This was a modern tower block of flats with four people sharing each flat; they had their own rooms and shared the bathroom and kitchen.

Les was very careful with her. He would come to her flat where they would chat, listen to music—they both enjoyed a wide variety from Pop, Frankie Lane, Oscar Peterson, especially Hymns to Freedom, and country music—they would sit on her bed with Les cuddling her for hours. Even her small room with a small light on could be very warm and relaxing.

One night, they were at Les' home. His mother was staying at her cousin's. They were snuggled up on the big comfy sofa, with music playing and the warm glow from the coal fire blazing away.

Les turned her face to his and kissed her gently. She was melting inside. She felt the familiar trembling that she had whenever he kissed her. She felt the urges that had become more frequent. She couldn't believe she felt this way. She had never had these urges before. She also knew she would have to let him know how she felt. He was afraid of upsetting her, so he wouldn't make the first move.

She turned to him and put her hand on his cheek. She noticed that for all he had was a dark shadow on his face. There were no whiskers to feel. He turned and kissed her again, but this time she held him close, and they kissed repeatedly. The feelings were so strong and all consuming. Les broke away and said he would make some coffee. Jo could see the tell-tale signs in his trousers.

'No, stay with me.' He hoped he could see the longing in her eyes.

'Are you sure, you know what's going to happen if we carry on like this? I'm trying to control myself, but it's very hard.'

'Les, I have never been surer of anything. We will be married some day, so stop worrying and let things happen.'

He sat down, held her close, and while kissing her, his hand stroked her breasts, and through her thin blouse, he could feel her nipples harden. He gently removed her clothes, and she helped him with his. She could see the admiration in his face as he looked at her naked body. He very gently touched the auburn hair that grew in an almost perfect triangle pointing the way for them to join in total pleasure. At the same time, he was teasing her nipples with his teeth. Jo thought she would burst. She even took him in her hands and gently massaged him until they could stand it no longer. As he gently parted her legs and entered her, she rose to him and cried out with pleasure, her body exploding with a vibrant fantastic pleasure like she had never felt before. They climaxed together, and she experienced the most exquisite ecstasy. She didn't want him to move. She had never felt this way before and didn't believe it was possible. Oscar Peterson's 'Hymns to Freedom' was playing, and Jo thought that was exactly how she felt.

They spent the weekend together, slept together, and made love several times. They had explored each other's bodies, and Jo felt she had learnt more about herself and making love than she had ever known. With his tenderness, Les had proved she wasn't frigid as she had believed from what Roy had said. Les had taught her that making love was a natural thing for two people as much in love as they were. He had broken down the remaining barriers. She had talked to him about all her fears and the things that had happened in her life. He was stunned; he had never experienced anything like it, but he was there for her and that was all she needed. As she was getting ready to go back to the Nurse's Home on the Sunday night ready for work on the Monday morning, she looked in the mirror, and said, 'Everyone will be able to tell what we've been doing. I can even see the difference in me.'

'You have no need to worry on that score. They will just be jealous,' he replied.

'I don't care. I feel so good.'

In bed that night, Jo remembered what a favourite great-aunt, who was widowed in the war and never remarried, had once said when Jo had asked her why she had never married again. 'Joanna, in this life, I firmly believe there is only one man for each woman, and Joe was mine. We were soul mates and no other man could make me feel like he did, so I live with my wonderful memories, and that is all I need.'

Jo now knew what she meant. It was on her mind so much, she had to get up, and she made a cup of tea, and then decided to put into words what she felt by writing Les a letter. She knew she would be seeing him that night, but somehow, she could put it on paper better than saying it.

Mr dearest darling Les,

I know this seems crazy, but I just wanted to put into words how I feel, and it is easier for me to write them down. I want you to know how much I love you, and I now realise how much you love me. For the first time in my life, I know what it means to be in love. I am so lucky to have found the most loving, caring, and gentlest man in the world. I will never forget last weekend. For a woman with 3 bairns I felt like a virgin. You proved to me how making love can only be that good if you love the person, and I do so very much. You may think this is silly, but I have written a poem for you. Please don't laugh at me. You have created this crazy woman in love.

As I sit here and watch the world go by,
Wonder about you and I,
I think of the love we have for each other,
And wait impatiently for you to discover,

That the love I have belongs to no other.

Forgive me my darling for feeling blue,

It's because of the lifetime I've spent without you,

Then suddenly every thing's bright,

When I think of our future and the stars we can watch shine
    at night.

I sit and look at my finger that's bare,

And dream of the ring you soon will put there, I hear the choir
    singing and feel the heavenly aura around us.

The church is full with people who care,

I look into your eyes and we are elsewhere,

The vicar says will you and we say we will.

Then now and forever we belong to each other,

We kneel and we pray to thank God for the day,

He brought us together.

I know that this means we will stay there forever,

Now I am to be your wife who will forever be part of your life.

Now you can see what a silly fool you are marrying. My only concern is you will never know the thrill of having children of your own. I want you to think about this again. You may say it doesn't matter, but you must think about it. I would hate you to regret it later.

You know in a weird way I am grateful to my past for showing me that I must value what I have now. I love you so very much, Les, the words aren't enough.

Yours forever remember
I love you, Jo [almost Williams] sounds good, eh. I am
practising my signature xxxxxxxxxxxxxx

A few days later, Jo received a letter from him. Love makes you do crazy things, like writing letters when you see each other almost daily.

My dearest darling Jo,

You must be crazy writing letters when we only parted that morning.

But please don't stop. It was fantastic to receive it in the morning post. I kept it with me all day and read it several times. How could I ever forget how much you love me, just as I will never stop loving you? Whenever I think of you [several times a day], I get this wonderful warm glow inside. I must show it on my face, but I don't care. I want everyone to know how much in love I am. I love the poem you wrote. I only wish I could write like that. But beautiful words like that could only come out of a beautiful person, and by that I mean inside as well as out. You will have to excuse my writing as I have never written any letters like this before. Unfortunately, due to your shifts, I, we, have to wait until Friday to see each other. I will come for you straight from work, but I will ring you every night. I miss you so much. I cannot wait to hear the church bells ringing, which will mean we will be together every day. I hope you can decipher my writing. It looks as if a spider has crawled all over the paper. I think the army has places you can send things for decoding. Maybe you should send this. Well, my darling, I will close for now. I hope this isn't too bad for the first attempt. You will have to judge. We must both be either crazy or in love. I wonder which ha ha. Goodnight and God bless.

All my everlasting love to the only girl in the world for me.

I love and miss you very much

Les xxxxxxxxxxxxxxxxxxxxxx

just the start of a lifetime of them

Chapter Forty-seven

Les had shown her that there were good men on this earth, and she had found that she trusted him completely; he looked after her very well. He was her best friend, and most importantly, she had finally seen that sex was not that; if it was with someone you love, it is making love, not just having sex. The hardest part of that day had been Roy. He had even managed to affect her wedding day. He had been funny about letting her see the children after hearing she had a boyfriend and had then at the last minute refused to let the bairns come to the wedding. Gail should have been a bridesmaid, and the boys, attendants. She had sent photos and cake, but later Gail had told her, he had thrown them away.

The wedding day dawned fresh with morning sun shine. The birds were singing. Jo was amazed how calm she felt, no nerves at all. The thoughts about her children kept forcing their way into her mind, but she tried hard to push them away. She would not let Roy spoil this very special day any more than he already had. There was a gentle tap on the bedroom door, and Babs put her head in.

'Oh, you have woken up then. Did you sleep well in a strange bed? Happy wedding day. I made you tea and toast. Is that enough or do you want a cooked breakfast? Mam's cooking one for the boys.'

Jo was getting married from her mam's pub.

'Well, thank you. Yes, I slept well, and tea and toast is enough for me. I will be sick if I eat more.' She sat up and took the tray from Babs.

'Today is the first day of the rest of my life, and it feels so good.'

'Well, you deserve it in spades, Jo. We are all so excited. Both Nannas are in the kitchen helping Mam with the food. She has gone over the top, Jo. Wait till you see it. They have done turkey beef pork and ham along with salmon, prawns, and even lobster. You just wait. Les' auntie has done a beautiful job on the cake. It looks magnificent. Do you know I can't remember when we were all together in the past? It must have been a long time ago. Even our Harry is here. I am so happy I think I'll burst, so how you feel I can't think. Now eat your toast, and our Lynne's running you a lovely bath.'

As she lay back on her pillows, she gazed at the beautiful wedding dress hanging on the wardrobe door. She hadn't felt right wearing white, so she had had it made especially for her. Her dad had insisted on the best dress she could find. He was so pleased to be giving her away. She had shared his pleasure buying the dress.

It had matched the clouds outside. It had three layers, firstly white silk, then pale blue silk, and finally, white organza that seemed to float like a fluffy white cloud. The bodice sleeves and hem, including the edging of the eight-foot train, were all covered in exquisite white lace, that belied it's delicate look by being heavy enough to hold the dress and train in place.

After a lovely long soak in the bath that had been perfumed with Rive Gauche, she lay on the bed and relaxed until her sisters came in to help her get ready. Babs brushed her hair, while Lynne did her make-up; she did this so well it looked as if she wasn't wearing any, but her skin looked wonderful and her big brown eyes shone very brightly, all of which complimented her natural beauty. Babs gathered her hair up from the front and sides then fastened it in place and dressed it with a silk gardenia, which coordinated with the headdress of silk gardenias and carnations that she fastened into place. The rest of her hair cascaded down her back. The natural curls and waves looked beautiful and natural, which was what Jo wanted.

'Oh, Jo, you are so lucky. I wish my hair was like yours,' said Babs and was echoed by Pat.

'I wouldn't have to suffer these things if it was,' Babs said pointing to the rollers in her hair.

When she was ready, Jo came out of the bedroom and met her dad on the landing. He gasped in surprise, and Megan stood there in awe of this beautiful girl in front of them. Daniel was looking at her with admiration in his young eyes.

'Eh, our Jo, you look really good. I don't mind having sisters if they look like you.'

Jo bent over and gave him a hug.

Her sisters were all fighting to stop the tears, looking at their sister who they knew had gone through a lot, although they didn't know just what. It was lovely to see her looking so happy.

Sam popped a bottle of champagne, and when they all had a glass, he proposed a toast 'to our Jo'.

'Our Jo', they all cried in unison.

The chauffer arrived in a 1920 White Model T Ford, especially for her and her dad.

Alison, Lynne, Babs, and Pat had already left in an Austin Sheerline; it was a good job the Model T had been built to carry seven people as the space was full with her dress.

With her three sisters and Alison in peacock blue bridesmaid dresses and Daniel and Luke in grey trousers, white shirts, and peacock blue waistcoats as her male attendants, they created a wonderful sight as they walked down the aisle. Even at this stage, Jo was thinking how Gail, Ben, and Tony would have looked if he had let them come.

Les turned to see her approach as he heard the wedding march playing; he couldn't believe this vision of beauty was going to be his wife in a very short while.

All the way through the service, they couldn't take their eyes off each other. The congregation were in no doubt they were very much in love.

Later, the vicar told them how a lot of couples look at him as they say their vows, and how it was very emotional seeing how they looked at each other as they went through the service.

The photos outside the church were taken, and then they had a few minutes to themselves as they travelled to the reception.

'I am the proudest man on earth today, and I really do love you Mrs Williams.' Jo couldn't answer as she was receiving her first real kiss of her marriage.

When they got back to the pub, Harry had ordered a chimney sweep for luck. The whole day was fabulous. All of her family was there. Val was very quiet, but Jo believed that was the only way she could handle things, especially with Harry there.

Jo was the happiest woman on earth when she finally climbed into bed with her husband. She felt as if this was the first time she had slept with a man, probably due to the fact she was in love with the most wonderful man on earth, as her aunt had said, the only man on this earth for her. They were a perfect match.

Chapter Forty-eight

They had lived with Les's mam for a few months until they had the deposit for a house, and in February 1975, they moved into their own home in Pontefract. Jo found it hard to believe she was not in rented property as she had been all of her life. She would almost run home from work to cook their teas, and her happiness would have been complete if she had her children.

There had been changes in the rest of the family as well. Harry and Lauren were expecting their first child, and they had a little girl Zoe in November that year and that was soon to be followed by tragedy.

Malcolm and Anne had had Jake in March 1975 and would have another son Joe the following year.

Babs was enjoying her work in paediatric nursing and was progressing very well. Pat had qualified in teaching the hard of hearing and would spend her life with children, and it looked as if neither of them would marry. But they both enjoyed their lifestyles, working with children. Val seemed to accept that her lot in life, which she did enjoy, was to look after Luke. She was totally devoted to him, and Archie understood he would always come second, but he accepted that. Her other children kept in touch, some more than others, and she seemed happier than she had ever been. Jo was even trying to forgive her for what she had done and continued to try to be close to her mum, but their relationship would never be as it should have been.

One evening at work, during visiting, she was having a coffee with the other ward staff when one of the ward sisters asked her when her baby was due. Jo laughed saying she was not pregnant, and the sister said she should do a test. Jo did the next morning and was ecstatic and shocked when it came back positive. When she told Les that night, they were beside themselves, and they rang their mums and all their friends to tell them the good news. Val and Archie had moved back to Hull, and they had been offered a pub there, which was much better as they couldn't settle outside of Hull

Jo had rung Jane, Roy's housekeeper, wondering if she would be able to see the bairns to tell them; however, Jane said Roy had forbidden this under any circumstances. She also said that he had agreed that now Jo was married they were to be married in August. Jo knew he had hit Jane and asked her if she was sure. She replied it wasn't so bad now he was much better. Jane agreed to tell the bairns in the kindest way she could

Two weeks later, when she was around twenty weeks pregnant she woke up in pain and was bleeding, Les took her to the hospital where they lost their little boy. Jo was then firmly convinced there was something in her that meant she would never have children in her home.

Chapter Forty-nine

In the July of that year, they received a letter from Jane on Roy's behalf, asking them to have the children for the six-week summer holiday. Jo rang her to ask why this turnaround had happened. Jane said she was having problems with Gail and Tony; they were continually playing up and saying she wasn't their mam. Ben was fine, and she had no problems with him, but the social worker had said that if they had a longer stay with Jo, they would see what it would be like living there, and it could help. Jo agreed they would collect them on the 29 July.

The summer break went well, even though Jo had to work some of it. They managed and had a wonderful break; she had almost convinced herself this was their future. At the end of the time, Roy had insisted they return to him, and they would talk about things. It did strike them as strange that Ben had said that if Gail and Tony lived with her he would live with his dad or vice versa. However, they thought this could be because Jane obviously doted on him, and as a child, he would relish the attention.

A week after they had gone home, Gail rang her at eight thirty on the Friday morning, saying she had run away and would never go back. Jo had no car as Les had taken it to work; therefore, she asked Gail to go to Jo's friend Pauline's and said she would ring her there. Les was out on a break down; he worked in a garage, and when she rang, his manager told her he would be gone for a couple of hours the only thing she could think of was to ask Pauline to put Gail on the train to Doncaster, and Jo could get the bus from Pontefract and meet her there. It was agreed that Pauline would bring her to Doncaster on the train. They did this, and she brought Gail home. What a sorrowful sight she was, for school she was dressed in clothes that were almost rags with holes in the elbows and much too big for her, her shoes were three sizes too big with paper stuffed in the toes. Apparently these had belonged to Jane's oldest daughter. Jo had rung Jane to tell her where Gail was, and Jane said she had already phoned the police, who would be calling there, which they did. But only to ask Gail if she had run away or had Jo taken her from her dad's and satisfied that it was on Gail's choice, he left. Two hours later, a policewoman came and said she needed to ask Gail some questions, and when Jo asked why, she was shocked to hear Jane had said Roy had interfered with her. Jo just couldn't get her head around this. He may have hit them, but she couldn't believe he would do that. When the policewoman asked Gail about the two instances, it turned out that in one instance, he had pinched her bottom when the whole family was waving goodbye to an uncle, and at another time, he had lifted her down the bed to retrieve her pillow that had fallen behind the headboard.

Before the police left, Jo warned her that if he asked for Gail to be returned to him, she wouldn't let her go, and the policewoman assured her this would not happen because of the allegations that had been made. Gail wondered if this was why Jane had said those things, so Gail would not be going back to them. She had said many times how she knew when Roy looked at Gail he was seeing Jo.

Gail settled in quite quickly, even asking Jo that first day if she could call Uncle Les Dad, and Jo told her this was her choice. When he had come home from work that night, Gail ran out and said, 'Hello, Dad.' He told Jo later that he had felt one hundred feet tall at her calling him Dad.

Tony was still having a lot of problems, but Jo's solicitor had told them they must sort custody of Gail out first, as it would be much harder to get Tony. Ben seemed settled, but Jane was paying him a lot of attention, and it was understandable that he would respond to her.

Eventually, they got custody of Gail, and were moving house when Jane rang up and what she said shocked Jo

'You can have Tony. When can you come for him?'

'How come, what's happened?' Gail was stunned

'I've told Roy, it's Tony or me. I can't take anymore, and he says come and get him.'

Jo didn't think of the impact this would have on Tony, his dad swapping him for his wife. She was just delighted to be told she could have him.

Jo had been ill and was told she needed a hysterectomy as she had a potentially cancerous condition. She was having the operation that week, and after the surgery, the surgeon had told them that it was the damage to her uterus, following Tony's birth and that meant it healed with adhesions and this meant she could never carry a baby to full-term, and once again, Roy had affected her happiness. It was agreed they would come for Tony in two weeks', and Jo felt she should be at home when he came.

She had developed septicaemia and was very ill; therefore, her stay in hospital was four weeks, but Gail had kept Tony informed of what was happening. When Jo came home, she was not well enough to travel; therefore, Les and Gail went for him. When they got back, Jo was thrilled. She had two of her children, a wonderful husband, and Ben seemed happy with Jane if not Roy.

Les told her the two of them had been chatting in the car, and Tony had asked Gail if he could call Les *Dad* as well, she said, of course, and now he had two children. Between them and Les' mam, they had replaced every stitch of clothing the two of them came with, which was an expensive exercise. But the new things were much better than what they had come with, so everyone was pleased. Roy had bought Tony a new bike for the previous Xmas, and Tony told Les his dad said he could only have his bike if he paid him for it. Les had said not to worry, and he would buy him a new one; it was October, so Xmas would soon be here again. He told Jo he would never put money in that man's hands.

They had been to court and got custody of Tony, so everyone was happy. Jo and Les were worried about money, and it had cost a fortune, buying all their clothes and paying for the solicitors; however, they could pay their mortgage and eat well, so they managed although saving money had to stop for quite a while.

A few months after Tony came to live with them, Jo and Les were sitting watching TV when Gail and Tony came into the room, and Tony switched the TV off and sat down.

'What are you doing, we were watching that?' said Jo.

'We want to ask you something,' said Gail. 'We want to know if Dad can adopt us. We want to be his kids and called Williams.'

'Wow, you two are full of surprises, but this one is a big one.' Les was shocked, amazed, puzzled, and a whole host of other emotions.

'What has made you think of this, and how do you know about adoption?' asked Jo.

'Oh, Mam, we aren't thick, you know, and we have been talking about it at school. We want Dad to be our dad proper, not him in Scunthorpe.'

'Well, we will have to start by talking to the solicitor to see if it is possible, then we will go from there. So don't go getting your hopes up as they may say it can't be done.'

Les had been deep in thought and looked at them both.

'I'm absolutely thrilled that you want this, and we will do our very best. But if it can't be done, remember in here,' he touched his heart, 'you are my children, and we can change your names by deed poll if needed, so leave it with us.'

The kids were delighted that something would be done. They left the room and went back upstairs to Gail's room to talk about it.

It did take time and a lot of effort, but eventually, they managed to get the adoption case to court. Roy had signed the papers, saying as long as it wasn't costing him any money it was fine by him. He wasn't there on the day, but a representative from his solicitors was. It was held in chambers with just the required people there. The judge was not happy despite the solicitor's arguments and Jo was certain he was going to say no, and her mind was in a whirl, trying to think of something when Gail spoke.

'Excuse me, sir, but if you don't let me be adopted, I can never get married.' Jo was shocked and so it seemed was the judge.

'How do you mean you can't get married? Would you explain that to me?' he asked.

'Well, I never want to be called Peterson again. This is my dad, and I want to be called Williams, so if I have to stay as Peterson, I will not get married.'

'I see, and what about you young man?' The judge looked at Tony, who with his usual shyness said, 'Gail is right, this is our dad, and we want it to be proper.'

Everyone was silent for a few minutes that seemed like forever and then the judge looked at each one of them.

'Well, I can't be responsible for you becoming a spinster, can I? Therefore, as there is no contact with Mr Peterson or his siblings, and the paternal grandparents are both deceased, then I had better grant the adoption, you are now Gail and Tony Williams, congratulations.'

They almost danced from the courthouse after thanking the judge and everyone else. Their solicitor had told them that if Gail had not spoken out he would not have granted the adoption; this proved that outspoken honesty was a good thing, sometimes.

Chapter Fifty

On August, Bank Holiday, Sunday morning, Jo was woken by a loud knocking on the front door, she woke Les, and they went downstairs, followed by Pete and Steve, who were staying for the weekend.

Les opened the door to find a policeman and woman on the doorstep, and after introducing themselves, they asked him if they could come in. Les stepped aside.

'Mrs Peterson?' asked the policeman.

'I used to be. It's Williams now. What's happened, is someone hurt? Is it my son?'

'Firstly, may we ask who everyone is?'

'Yes, of course, this is my husband Les, and this is my brother Pete and his friend Steve, will you please tell me what's wrong.'

'Yes, please sit down, all of you,' PC Watson said. The four of them squashed together on the settee, and the two police sat in the armchairs.

'You know Mr Roy Peterson.'

'Of course, I was married to him.'

'Well, I'm afraid, we have some bad news, Mr Peterson is in hospital. He was badly beaten last night, and it is suspected he may not walk again.'

Jo felt the room spin and she grabbed Les's arm. Steve got up and headed for the kitchen, telling them he would make some coffee.

'What about my son, Ben, is he all right?' was the first thing Jo asked.

'He's fine and seemed quite happy with his stepmother. Now could I ask about your whereabouts last night?'

Les answered, 'We went to the local after dropping the children off at my mother's, then we went to the Talk of Yorkshire, which is a night club in Bradford, we got back here about three o'clock this morning.'

Steve came back in with a tray of coffees, which were gratefully received.

'Have you any idea who did it?' asked Pete.

'Not really, he was on his way home from the local, when he was attacked. A witness said they thought they saw a man in a sailor's uniform running away from the scene.'

PC Watson noticed the look that passed between them and asked if they knew anything more.

'No, it's just that we have a brother in the navy, but he lives in Portsmouth,' said Pete.

'Is he in this country or at sea?'

'I aren't sure. He was away, but I don't know where he is now.' Jo agreed with Pete, and said she didn't know where Harry was.

The police took their leave saying they may have to call again, later. Jo said she would ring Jane and check how things were.

As the police left, Jo looked at Pete.

'He wouldn't would he? Our Harry wouldn't do that.' She looked at him for reassurance.

'No, of course not, our Harry would never hurt anyone like that. Although I must admit, he was very angry over what Roy has put you through, but no he wouldn't do that.'

Jo rang Jane who was obviously upset, but reassured her that Ben and she were fine. She said the doctors couldn't say how Roy would be until he regained consciousness, and she would keep Jo informed so she could tell Gail and Tony.

Jo had mixed feelings about everything. She had hated Roy, but now her life was so different she had pushed the hate out of her system and accepted that if she hadn't been married to him, she wouldn't have her wonderful children, who didn't seem that bothered when she told them what had happened, and it was as if he had never been their father.

They sat around the table with coffee and toast, once again made by Steve, trying to work things out.

'I am worried about our Harry. Should I ring and see if he is at home?'

'No, Jo, leave it for now. The police will be in touch with him, and if he isn't there, it will worry Lauren and remember she is due soon, so let's wait for them to contact us, and if needed, Steve and I will go down there.'

'Now think about this. It isn't supposed to be anything to do with what he did to you, Jo. He played around with other women, didn't he? He is a nasty person and may have upset someone in the pub. It could be anything, and to be honest, I wish it had been me that gave him what he deserved, and I would like to shake the hand of whoever it was.' Les was upset at how this had spoiled Jo's happiness, and they had been having a wonderful weekend.

'Yes, you're right, of course, you are, but do you think we could go and see Ben. I need to know he is all right, and we could ring your mam and make sure Gail and Tony are all right too.'

'OK, get ready, and we will have a ride to Sunny Scunny. Will you two stay here until we get back?' Les asked Pete.

'Of course, we will stay again tonight and play it by ear, and as to when we go home, I'll ring Dad, and he will sort out work and things for us.'

Chapter Fifty-one

They had rung Jane to make sure visiting was all right. They had told Les's mam, but asked her not to say anything to the bairns, and they would call on the way home and tell them themselves. There may be more news by then.

They seemed to arrive quite quickly, maybe because there was so much going through their heads, and in no time at all, they turned into the Council Estate were Roy lived. Les's car, Ford Cortina 1600 E, looked out of place here, and there were very few cars about. Supposedly, people couldn't afford them.

Jo had never noticed before how the Council had built all the houses exactly the same, and the only thing that differed was the colour of the front door, but the colours were repeated along each street. Les drove very carefully as there were a lot of children playing in the street. Jo wondered how safe it was to let bairns, some of whom looked no more than three or four years old out in the street. She was also fascinated they didn't catch colds or flu as they were skimpily dressed, for although it was the end of August, there was quite a nip in the air, as if autumn was coming early, but she supposed they kept warm running around with their balls or skipping. The boys were playing football and were calling each other by famous footballers' names. She heard someone call out for Georgie Best. Surely, that isn't his real name, she thought to herself.

Jane opened the door before they had chance to knock, greeting them and inviting them in. She told them to go through to the lounge while she made some tea. Ben had gone to the hospital with his uncle Terry, but had rung to say he was on his way home.

'How are you coping?' Jo asked Ann. 'Do you want us to take you to the hospital?'

'No, I'm fine. I saw him this morning. He is going to be all right, and he seems to be coming round, and the doctors are very optimistic.'

Jo was thinking that if it had been Les, she would not have left him, when Jane said, 'It will do him good to feel some hurt. It might make him realise what he has done to you and me. I'm sure you can understand that.'

'Of course, I can, but I thought, he was better with you.'

'Oh yes, he has been, but that doesn't mean he has stopped, and I still think he is seeing other women, although I can't prove it.'

'Well, why are you still here, if things are so bad.'

'Because daft as it sounds, I still love him, and when things are good, we have a beautiful relationship. He does support us all, and he gives me very good housekeeping money and takes me out every Saturday night. He is getting better, and who knows one day he may stop altogether.'

'I do understand, Jane. I have had similar thoughts, but I am just worried about who did it. The police said someone saw a sailor running away, and I have a brother in the navy.'

'Well, if it was him, I would like to shake his hand, but I don't think it was. I am sure he was seeing a woman from a couple of streets away, and her husband is in the navy, too.'

Les felt as if he should give them time alone to talk about their feelings; therefore, he excused himself and went into the kitchen to make some coffee. He deliberately took his time to give them some space.

Jo was deep in thought and didn't notice him leave, and Jane continued.

'I know you understand because he did the same to you, didn't he? Oh, he was wonderful, at first. I fell in love with him right from the start, and I was only here two days before we were sharing a bed. I was so in love, or so I thought, that I even accepted it when he kept telling me that when you came back, I was out the door. I just prayed you wouldn't come back.'

'Don't blame yourself, Jane. I would have done the same as you. I think, I was so young, only sixteen. I couldn't see where I was going, and I fully understand how you feel. I only wish whoever did this didn't finish him off. It would be so good to feel completely free of him, but then there are the children to think of especially Ben, and Gail used to be so close to him. I think she would feel it. It's crazy to think he is still in the background when I am married to such a wonderful man. I love Les so much, and I now know what love really is, but the things Roy did are always there.'

Jo didn't realise that Les could hear her, and she never gave it a thought, but standing in the kitchen, he was seething. He went outside for a cigarette, and he was wishing it had been him who gave Roy what he deserved. Only he would have made sure he finished the job. These were savage thoughts from someone who was such a gentle man. He noticed he only had three cigarettes left, so he walked to the end of the street to the garage where he bought 100. He thought he may need them before this day was over. When he got back, he realised, they had not even noticed he had gone. They were talking about the things they had in common, and Les did think this would probably do them both good. They had stopped crying and were talking calmly, so he made the coffees and rejoined them.

Jane was telling Jo about herself.

'Yes, I'm from a place called Norton near Stockton. I was a teacher there, but I moved down here when my first husband left me. I saw his advert for a housekeeper, applied, and here we are. I have thought about going back, but I would have to live with my parents, which isn't easy with kids. I don't know if I could cope alone, and I would hate to leave Ben. I'm sorry, Jo, but I love him like he was my own, and Roy has been fairly good with him so far. I think that's because he hasn't got Gail and Tony. Oh, I nearly forgot, the policeman who has been dealing with all this said to say hello to you. He knew you when you were here, now what's his name.'

'Is it Browning?'

'Yes, that's it, Sergeant Browning. He said he knew you.'

'He was the one who got me out when Roy attacked and stabbed me; he was really supportive and helped me a lot.'

Les was shocked he had asked the many times where the scar on her back was from, but she would change the subject so he had stopped asking, respecting her privacy.

'Why didn't you tell me?' asked Les as he moved over and sat on the chair arm in order to put his arms round Jo's shoulders.

'What kind of an animal is he? I would have dealt with him if I'd known about that. How he manages to charm women like he does, I will never know.' He looked at both of them, trying to understand.

'I wish I could explain what kept me here, and why I came back to him, but I can't. I know only too well what it's like being the child of a broken marriage, and I swore not to put my bairns through that, and I was terrified of being on my own. I thought, he would kill me if he had found me, and I didn't tell you because I knew what your reaction would be. I love you so much I didn't want you going to prison because of him. I could not live without you.' They kissed not even thinking about Jane.

'For me, I didn't want to admit what a fool I had been. I knew I had made a terrible mistake, but I wanted it to work, so I stayed in the hope it would work out, and as I have said, I really love Ben. I know he is your son, but he feels like my own. You know, Roy still says he loves you, until you and Les got married, he really thought you would come back and that's why we got married in the August after you two did it in the May. He said you wouldn't come back, so we could be married, and I accepted it.'

'Do you know at one point, I almost did. I was missing the bairns so much. I actually came here, but when I was stood thinking about it, you two came into the kitchen and looked so close. I walked away.' Jo reflected.

'Well, thank God, I did something right. If you had come back, you would have been trapped forever, that is if he didn't kill you. No, Jo, you did the right thing.'

The back door opened and Ben came in with Roy's brother, Terry. He came over to his mother and gave her a kiss, then went to Jane, and he sat on the settee with her.

'How's your dad, son?' asked Jo.

Terry answered her, 'He is going to be all right. Unfortunately, he has a couple of cracked ribs and a lot of cuts and bruises, but other than that OK, and he will be home in a few days, Jane, so what are you going to do?'

'What choice do I have? Of course, I will stay here. You never know. This might have taught him a lesson, and we could be all right.' She held Ben's hand and said, 'We'll be good, won't we, son?'

'Of course, we will, and I am getting bigger and therefore, he might stop if he thinks someone else is watching out for you. Uncle Terry has told him he will get more of the same if he hits you again, and I think he has frightened him. He did ask me what Nanna had said, and he knows she thinks he got his just rewards, cos Uncle Terry told him that.'

Jo could see they were going to be all right, and she had to admit defeat when she saw how close Ben and Jane were. She could accept that because he seemed so happy. Maybe he preferred to be the only one rather than one of three, and as much as it hurt she said her goodbyes and they left.

Chapter Fifty-two

Harry was sitting at a table in the Travel Lodge on the M1, and he had pulled into the Leicester Mark field services at Junction 22. He was deep in thought, trying to think what he should do now.

He had intended to surprise Jo and spend the weekend with them. He knew Pete and Steve would be there and looked forward to a good weekend. He had driven from Portsmouth late that night after Lauren had gone to her mum's for the weekend. He had borrowed his mate's car, a Maxi, which was comfortable to sleep in, so he had pulled off the motorway and parked in a lay-by to grab some sleep and was amazed when he slept until eight in the morning. He had a drink from his flask, which was surprisingly still warm and then he set off again, stopping at the services to freshen up. He decided to go to Scunthorpe first to see if he could see Ben. At least, he could tell Jo how he was. After breakfasting at a transport cafe, he finally arrived at their house; he parked in a cul-de-sac opposite the house where he could watch for Ben. Children were playing cowboys and Indians in the street, and he was intrigued how children always seemed to enjoy that game. He remembered doing like these kids, using two pegs, slotting one into the other to make a pretend gun. These kids were using old coat hangers with a bit of string across as a bow and twigs as arrows, and they were having a great time.

Roy came into the front garden. He was obviously mad at something as he was shouting at Ben. Although Harry couldn't hear what was being said, it was obvious he was giving him hell over something.

He stayed there for hours, and Roy appeared to be in a mood all day, and as dark was coming in, they had turned the kitchen light on, and he saw Roy slap Jane across the face. He was furious, the bastard, why do some men get such a kick out of hurting women and kids.

He had to go and find somewhere to eat, and he needed a toilet, so he left vowing to return. He remembered there was a pub round the corner, and it was quarter to five, and it opened at five, so he decided to go there. After eating his steak pie and chips and drinking his lager, he got up and went to the bar to order another pint.

'Do you live round here?' the barmaid asked him. 'I don't think, I know you, do I?'

'No, I live miles away. I was in the area, so I thought, I would look up a friend of a friend. I thought he came in here.'

'Oh yes, what's his name?'

'Roy Peterson, do you know him by any chance?'

'Count yourself lucky, he is only a friend of a friend. You don't need to know people like him.'

Harry was amazed how outspoken she was.

'What makes you say that? I don't actually know him that well.'

'He is the worst kind of bastard that walks this earth if you ask me, the way he treats his family is disgusting, and I knew his first wife. She used to work here, you know. Well, he nearly killed her, and now he is at it again with this one.' She was drying glasses as she spoke. 'I finish here tonight for two weeks holiday, and I can't wait, I hate even serving him. He thinks he is God's gift to women, he does.'

'Going anywhere nice on your holiday,' he wanted to keep her talking, but tried not to be too obvious.

'Yes, I'm so excited and scared. We fly from Manchester to Corfu on the 8.00 a.m. flight tomorrow. I've never flown before, and I am scared stiff.'

'Can't say, I blame you. As you can see, I'm in the navy, and I prefer water to sky any day.'

She laughed and told him that Roy lived across the road on the right Number 38 if he wanted to see him; she also said he would be in the pub by eight o'clock till closing as normal.

'You know, I don't like speaking ill of anyone, but he is a savage, Jo. His first wife was always battered, and he had stabbed her as well, and this wife Jane she is called. Well, she always has black eyes and such. She even had a miscarriage when she was five months gone, and said she had fallen downstairs. That's just what Jo said when she lost her twins and nearly lost her youngest, Tony.'

She leant over the bar, which was quiet, but she obviously didn't want anyone to hear her.

'That bairn nearly died along with his mum, and he didn't even bother to go and see her. His women are prone to falling downstairs, or that's what they want folk to believe.'

'Well, I think I will give this visit a miss, and I'm driving, so I've had enough to drink, nice chatting to you and enjoy your holiday. Have a little drink in the airport and that will help your nerves.' He picked up his topcoat and took his leave.

He was sitting on the park bench. The street lights gave the flowers a different look, and the roses had a lovely perfume that was very strong, the fuchsias were full of flowers that danced in the breeze and looked like little lanterns, or even miniature ballerinas with a variety of coloured skirts on. He sat thinking about what he had learnt, and his surroundings barely made an impression. He didn't even remember walking here from the pub. He was deep in thought, thinking about the mistakes he had made in his life.

Thinking about his father, and it really hurt him to think he was his father, not Sam, but what he had done to Jo, and as he later found out, to Pat as well, and she was his daughter. If he had done something earlier, he could have stopped a lot of suffering. He didn't even think about the fact he had been a small boy back then. Anyway, he had sorted Jim out. It had been an accident, but Harry knew Jim would have died that night if he hadn't fallen in the dock. He would not have let him walk away. Now it was Roy's turn.

He went back to the pub and sat quietly in the corner of the snug, which was next to the bar. The barmaid from earlier was no longer there. She must have got off early. He was in a good position, and he could hear what was said but not be seen. Roy sounded as if he was trying to buy friends, and he could hear his voice over everything.

'Hi, Jim, let me get you a pint.'

'Hello, Bill, pint of bitter, is it?'

'Bob back home again. Long trip, this time. Do you want a pint of bitter as usual with a whiskey chaser?'

This went on for another hour until the landlord called time, and Harry had noticed that it seemed as if no one had bought Roy a drink. Roy was the last to leave the bar, and Harry followed him out, instead of going via the footpath Roy took an alley down the side of the garage, and Harry followed him. It was very dark down there. Roy seemed to realise someone was behind him, and he turned.

'Who's there? Come into the light so I can see you.' He moved to where a streetlight cast a glow.

Harry stepped forward.

'I know you, you're that cock sucking little whore's brother, aren't you? Poor little Joanna, the lying little . . . '

His words were cut short as Harry's fist hit him in the face, and once he started he couldn't stop. The years of frustration had finally erupted and the blows were coming thick and fast, blood was pouring downs Roy's face and his eyes were closing, his nose was obviously broken, and one of his teeth had come out. He cowered in a heap on the floor, crying.

'No more, please, don't hit me again. I'm sorry for what I said about Jo. I do still love her. Please, no more.' He was cowering with his hands over his head, sitting on the floor.

Harry realised what he was doing, and what a coward Roy was. This was an unfair fight, so he turned and started walking away. As he did, he heard a grunting noise behind him, and he turned just in time to see a knife blade heading his way. He moved sideways and grabbed Roy's arm, twisting it up his back, causing him to drop the knife. He hit him again and again, until he crumpled into an unconscious heap on the floor. He picked up the knife to get rid of it, so he couldn't use it on anyone else, and gave him a savage kick to his back and walked away. He heard a woman's footsteps approaching, so he turned and ran to his car and drove away. It's just as well there was no police around or he would have been in real trouble. Speeding and being covered in Roy's blood, just before he reached the motorway, he pulled into a lay-by. He reached into the backseat to retrieve his kitbag, where he found a pair of jeans, a T-shirt, and jumper. Changing his top clothes in the car, he then opened the door to change his trousers. He found a carrier in the back of the car, and he put his uniform in it, tied it up, and threw it into a small river that was running nearby. The clothes were heavy and they eventually would drag the bag down. He realised he must get back to Portsmouth as soon as he could. No one, not even Lauren knew he was here, so maybe he would get away with it. He would just have to deny anything Roy said, and in any case, he had a pal who would swear he had been with him all night.

When he got home, he thought about things and wondered how he would deal with it if the police believed Roy. He knew he could never go to prison. The children's home had been bad enough, but he had become used to the feeling of space you get at sea. He didn't even know if Roy would be all right, what if he died? That would be what he deserved, but Harry was worried about the repercussions. He decided he would wait and see what happened and then he could always get away if necessary. He didn't want anyone else to get the blame, so he decided to write a letter to the only solicitor he had an address for.

Dear Mr Oxon,

If you are reading this, then I have left the country, but I want to clear up any mess I have left behind. Firstly, let me explain who I am. My name is Harold Downie. You helped my sister Joanna who was Peterson then. My name should not have been Downie as my mother's second husband was really my father, but I prefer not to even go down that road.

I have given you no return address for obvious reasons. I know I should be honest and take the punishment for what I have done. But after spending some time in a children's home and then joining the Royal Navy I could not cope with being incarcerated in any prison. Now for the reason, I am writing this. Firstly, I am responsible for the death of my mother's second husband Jim. He did fall into the dock, and it was by accident, but I was there and goaded him until he was frightened of what I would do, took a step backwards and fell. I don't know for sure whether he died before he hit the water, but I walked away and left him. He was supposed to be my stepfather, but was really my father, and I am bitterly ashamed of that fact. I cannot go into details as others would be hurt if I did, but suffice to say he was a paedophile abusing little girls and deserved to die.

Secondly, my sister Joanna's first husband Roy Peterson, I don't know for sure, if he is still alive, but in any case, he was badly beaten up in an alleyway behind the garage at the end of the road where he lives. That was me; I followed him from the pub and gave him a good hiding. I did then try to walk away, but he came at me with a knife. I got it away from him, but then lost it completely and really beat him very badly. He was unconscious when I left him. I disposed of the knife in a skip so he could hurt nobody else with it.

I then went home to Portsmouth, where I arranged an alibi, but if you talk to the barmaid in the pub where Roy drinks called the Pied Piper, I don't know her name, but she flew to Corfu that night and was away for 2 weeks; ask her about the sailor she was talking to. Also as I was walking away, I heard a woman's footsteps, and I ran past her. I set off home and just before I joined the M62, at the Goole junction, heading for the M1, I pulled into a lay-by, where I changed my clothes and tied my uniform in a carrier bag, which I threw into a nearby river.

Please tell my family, I am very sorry. I never meant anyone to get hurt even though the two of them deserved it, and please tell them all I love them dearly.

Yours Sincerely,
Harry Downie

He then put into the envelope the letter he had written with the address of the solicitors in Hull. He hid it safely in his kitbag, ready for if he had to leave, suddenly. Lauren left him to sort his bag, as she was never sure what he wanted for each trip. He put the bag into his car, where he kept it ready for going to sea, and away from prying eyes.

Chapter Fifty-three

A few days later, he was driving to his ship along a dual carriageway, his mind was still all over the place, and he knew from Jo that Roy would eventually be OK. He was still thinking about what he would do if Roy sent the police after him.

He noticed a Ford escort in front of him that had started to swerve about, and it seemed the driver had lost control and then it hit the central barrier, balancing on two wheels it rolled over the barrier and landed on its roof.

Harry put his hazard lights on, then jumped out of his car, and ran over to the car, the lady driver had a nasty wound on her head and was bleeding heavily. She was also unconscious, and in the passenger seat, was a little girl about nine and in the back, was a little boy about five with a carrycot containing a baby next to him. They were all strapped in and seemed to be unhurt although the three of them were crying very loudly and made Harry think maybe there were injuries he couldn't see. He couldn't open the driver's door, so he cleared the broken glass from the window, released her seat belt and pulled her through the opening; he carried her on the hard shoulder behind his car and gently laid her on the grass, using his coat as a pillow. He ran back to the car and released the two older children, they were screaming in fear as he grabbed them one under each arm and ran back to his car with them, he thought this was the safest place, he put them in the back of the car, closed the door and ran back for the baby.

As he ran across the carriageway a lorry pulled up and the driver had blocked the road with it and put his hazards on, and then shouted out of the window. 'I have radioed for police and ambulance, what do you want me to do?'

'Tell them, there is a badly injured lady and three children who seemed to be shocked, but all right. I've put two of them in my car, and I'm just going for the baby.'

By this time, he was climbing into the car through the window, and he took the baby from the carrycot. It was very young about three weeks, he guessed. He pulled the neck of his jumper down, and tucked the baby in there to protect it from the broken glass everywhere. As he got out of the car, he saw the driver heading his way and pointing up the road, a jaguar sports car was heading his way very fast, in a split second he thought he must have swerved around the lorry, then he saw a cigarette in the driver's hand. He pulled the baby out of his jumper, looked at the lorry driver who nodded, and he threw the baby, thanking God the chap caught it, the sports car driver threw his cigarette out without thinking. Harry was trying to get out of the way, there was petrol everywhere, this had all happened in a very few minutes that seemed like forever to Harry.

There was an almighty explosion; the jaguar rose up in the air before crashing back down, throwing the driver out into the carriageway.

Fred Watkins, the lorry driver, stood in shock, cuddling the baby without thinking, and watched the car burn.

The police arrived at that point closely followed by the ambulance.

The police ran over to Fred.

'What's happened here, is everyone out of the car?'

'I don't know. I arrived after the accident, I tried to block the road, but that bloody idiot came through and threw a bloody cig-end out of his car. I saw a baby fly through the air at me, the last thing the poor sod did was save these babies lives. He must have played rugby or something the way he threw the baby. There is a woman over there on the banking, and two kids in the car over there, and this baby here.'

He was handing the baby to a policewoman.

'There was another bloke who got them all out of the car. I haven't seen him since it blew up, where the hell is he, he saved them all.'

The fire brigade had arrived and were putting out the fire. The ambulance people had got the mother and her children into the ambulance, while they waited for another one to get through the heavy traffic that had built up.

Fred was sitting in the ambulance obviously in shock. He had taken his jacket off because he had rolled it on to his stomach to protect the baby, and the back of his jacket was smouldering. The police came back to him, and told him what he already knew that the man who had saved this family had died.

Once the ambulances had left, and the police were clearing the scene, a constable came over to the sergeant and said, 'I found this letter in the kitbag in the Maxi. It must have belonged to the chap who died. He was in navy uniform.'

The sergeant took the letter, thinking it maybe a will, seeing how it was addressed to a solicitor. He put it in his pocket until later.

Chapter Fifty-four

As Jo stood by Harry's grave, she was thinking of the terrible things that had happened, and the lady and her children had made a speedy recovery, and had written a wonderful letter thanking the family for having such a brave man. He had saved all of her children, and she would never let them forget what he did.

'You will break that if you're not careful,' said Les, approaching her.

'Hello, love, I didn't hear you coming.'

'You were miles away. You should be careful. You are going to break your brooch,' he replied to her and put his arms around her.

'Did you know our Harry bought me this years ago in Beverley. Forget-me-nots, isn't that a coincidence or did he know he wouldn't grow old?'

'No, darling, it was just a nice thought. He loved you a great deal, you know, as do all your family and especially me. You have been here every day for the last five weeks, Jo. I'm worried about you. We can remember Harry anywhere. You don't have to come here.'

'I know, it was so good of Lauren to let us bury him next to my nanna and granddad, and she says she is thinking of selling up and moving here so that Zoe can have family around her. It's a shame Lauren has lost her mum and has no family of her own, but she is like another sister to me, so maybe that will help her cope.'

Les tried to lead her away from the grave, but she pulled away.

'Jo, come and sit here on this bench. You can still see the grave, and I have brought a flask of coffee. We have all the time in the world, my mam has the bairns, and they are all OK. Please come and sit down.'

They sat and drank the coffee; Jo emptied the dregs of her cup on the grass.

'I need to talk, Les. I need to get things of my chest, and my mind is in such a whirl.'

'You talk, my love. I will sit here and listen. Come and cuddle up to me, then you will be warm and maybe relax a little.'

'Will it ever stop? How much more pain can we take? The secrets my family has kept all of these years, first with Jim and what he did, first to me, and then our Pat. Do you know that's why I think she isn't interested in men? I have talked to her, and our Babs has tried, but to be honest, I think them two will carry on living together and never marry, and that's down to Jim. Maybe that affected how I was with Roy. Maybe, I wasn't the wife I could have been. Oh! Don't worry, I'm not saying what he did was my fault, but maybe it did affect our relationship especially in the beginning, then this, our Harry we got off to a bad start as kids, but then became very close I loved him so much you know. He always blamed himself. He said he had seen Jim in my room and did nothing, but he was only a bairn. He wasn't to blame, but that could be part of what sent him off the rails and caused him to have to go into that home. He had no childhood, then going to sea so young. I know he loved it, but he didn't have a family life. Mam drove him mad. She was so possessive and clinging, then when things finally come good, he marries and has a beautiful daughter. Everything to live for then this happens, why was he on that road, it's not fair.'

She cried on Les's shoulder and because he knew words wouldn't help he said nothing. She had to get it out of her system.

'Then what he did to Jim. I know he didn't push him, but he caused it to happen. Then Roy it seemed he had to compensate and get them back for what they did to me. I don't think he had planned that. I think that was a mixture of an accident and self-defence, and it was no more than what he deserved. I feel cheated that they wouldn't let anyone see him after he died. I know he would have been in a state, but I wanted to say goodbye.' The tears Jo had been fighting came now and she would feel better later.

Les hugged her close.

'Look, Jo, let's get this into perspective. Firstly, you are not to blame for what happened when you were kids. That is in the past and should stay there. You have suffered enough for that, and at least you and your mam can talk now. I will never understand what you went through no one could. Babs and Pat are very close and completely devoted to their work and are probably quite happy. Not everyone has to be married. The rest of your brothers and sisters have done well, and your mam is totally devoted to Luke. Pete has talked to me about your childhoods. Why he went to your dad's, and how Harry felt you know they were very close, and as Pete said your mam and Jim would never have coped when he came out, he wouldn't have met Steve and wouldn't be as happy as they are. Remember the two ladies, who came to Harry's funeral from that home, they must have thought a lot about him. He loved the sea, and he loved you. The main thing to take from this is how he died, Jo. He saved that lady and her children. He didn't die in vain. He died doing good things, and he gave his life for others. That's the most anyone can do. You saw that family at his funeral. They will never forget what he did for them. They even told me they are going to try for another baby next year, and if it is a boy, he will be called Harry, and a girl will be called Harriet, so he will live on in their minds, and remember, he died as he lived putting others first. Even the police closed the case after reading the letter he left for Mr Oxon, and remember, the tributes his pals and commanding officers paid to him at his funeral. All that proves what a man he was. We should think of that and carry the good memories and leave the bad ones behind. Don't let the people who hurt you then carry on doing that now.'

Jo stood up and took his hand in hers.

'You're right. He wouldn't have wanted me to be like this. We have a good life, and now it's time to look forward. I will come once a week and talk to Harry, telling him what's happening although I know he will be watching over us.'

They walked home hand in hand.

Chapter Fifty-five

1980

'Dad, can I have a lift to the Youth Club, please, and can we pick Debbie and Tracy up on the way,' Gail shouted from her bedroom.

'No, you can't. I need Dad to run me up to the Sports Centre. I'm playing squash at seven tonight. I've arranged it with Dean, Frank, and Sean, and we are practising for the tournament,' Tony answered before Les could say anything.

'Hey, you two, do I have a say in this. What if your mam and me were going out?' Les was climbing the stairs as he spoke.

'Dad, please, Mum and you won't be going out tonight. She is on the late shift, pretty, pretty please.'

They all laughed at Gail's persuasive pleas.

'Come on, get your things, I can take you both, but how are you getting home?'

'Could you pick me up, please?' asked Tony.

'I'm OK, Debbie's dad is fetching us home,' Gail answered.

'I will be pleased when one of you gets to seventeen and passes their driving tests. I should set up a business called Dad's Taxis.'

Tony laughed.

'You let the women in this family run rings round you, Dad. You won't catch me doing that.'

Gail came downstairs, looking as beautiful as ever.

'Oh, look, she has nicked my leather jacket again,' Tony complained half heartedly.

Les was laughing and said, 'What was that about women running rings around me and not you.'

Jo came home about nine thirty that night, and they had a wonderful peaceful half hour before Gail arrived. Tony had rung to say he was stopping over at Dean's if that was OK.

Gail was chattering about her good night at the Youth Club, and a boy called Martin kept coming into the tale. Les and Jo looked at each other wondering if they should be keeping an eye on her.

Chapter Fifty-six

'Happy Birthday, Zoe. Are you having a good time?'

'Yes, fank you, Auntie Jo, and fank you, for the new dress and shoes. They are gorgeous.'

For a six-year-old, she was more into clothes than toys. The only doll she played with was her tiny tears, which she called Morag as she loved her grandma. Lauren had moved here after Harry died, and she seemed to be well-settled and coping with the help of the family. Zoe ran off to help her auntie Lynne feed her twins, Laura and Glenn, who at just over a year old were a real handful.

'Now tell us what presents you got for your birthday?' asked Lynne as they were feeding the babies in their highchairs.

'Mummy bought me a new bike. It's pink and has ribbons flying off the handles. Did you know, I don't need them balancing fingers. I can ride wivout 'em. I am a big girl now aren't Auntie Lynne.'

'You certainly are, sweetheart, and a clever girl as well. Look how Laura is eating all her dinner. You are a big help to me feeding her for me.'

Jo was laughing with Lauren; they were wondering when Zoe would learn to say the 'th' sound. They agreed she would get it right eventually, and they were both thinking how proud Harry would have been of his daughter.

Jo was laughing and trying to find a way of keeping all the children happy. She was pleased they had moved into a big four-bedroom house, as trying to fit everyone in was difficult.

Pete was here with Steve, Malcolm, and Annette had brought Jake and Jo. Babs was here helping Pat with the three children they were fostering. Pat only worked part-time now they had taken up fostering. They had already had five other children on short-term stays, but Dawn, David, and Donna were sisters and brother that they had had for over two years now. If they thought they could they would have applied to adopt them, but didn't want to jeopardise having them staying with them. Dawn was ten, David eight, and Donna was only three years old. Only Dawn could remember a little of their mum, and apparently, they all had different dads, who were not involved at all. There was Lauren with her Zoe, and Lynne with her twins, her husband was busy and couldn't make it. Val had come to the party with Luke, but they weren't staying as Luke needed his bed with cot sides and other equipment now. As he got older, his condition deteriorated, and at twenty he was a big lad, and this put more strain on his heart, which was already affected by the Downs. The whole family knew they wouldn't have him for much longer, and they all tried hard to make his life as happy as possible. Luke was always happy and loving, and he beamed whenever one of them gave him a hug.

All in all, with ten adults and ten children in the house it was overflowing. Eventually, all the older children went outside to play, and Les had made the garden secure and put up a swing and slide set. They also had a couple of balls and skipping ropes, and Dawn was watching Donna, as she always did. Pat said she thought, Dawn was used to being 'mother' and Lynne's two were having a sleep. Gail and Tony as the oldest were very good at keeping an eye on the little ones and offering sweets and drinks when needed.

This meant the adults could have a coffee in peace.

Lynne came downstairs laughing, and she said, 'It looks like a dormitory up there. It's a good job you did the loft conversion, or we would never have fit everyone in. Those camp beds look good enough to sleep on.'

'I love having you all here. I only wish our Harry was here as well. I still miss him as I'm sure you all do, especially you, Lauren.'

'Yes, I do, but it is over three years ago, and those old sayings are right time does heal. In fact, I should tell you all something. I have started going out occasionally with a neighbour's son Patrick. It's early days yet, and I don't know if it will go anywhere, but I thought you should know.' She looked edgy.

'I'm sure I'm talking for us all,' said Pete. 'I think that's great and about time. Our Harry would not want you to be alone forever and good for you.'

The nods and smiles all round demonstrated how everyone agreed. The conversation carried on with general matters and then Les told them all how proud he was of his beautiful daughter Gail.

'Do you know she even got ten GSCEs and is staying on to take four A levels. She is very good at languages and taking English, French, German, and Russian, then wants to continue at university. Eventually, she wants to work as some sort of interpreter, and Tony is top of his class. He wants to be a doctor and is working hard for that. And did you know that Ben has also gained nine GSCEs and is going to college, although he hasn't decided what he wants to do, but he does want to be in some sort of business. He says things are good at home. Roy is much calmer, and he loves being with Jane.'

'Do you see much of him?' asked Malcolm.

'No, not really. He is worried about making Roy angry and it still does happen. He is very happy and as long as he rings up fairly often as he does. Jo is coping, aren't you, love?'

'Yes, so much as happened. I just have to accept what he wants, and we are lucky really when you look how things have turned out. All but our Harry that is, I still think about that letter he left, don't you?'

'Yes, we do, but even the police thought it was no good doing anything about any of it, and if truth be known it could have been any of us.' Pete looked around the men in the room 'that could have done what he did.'

'Did you know that the Musgrave family keeps in touch? They had another two children, Harry first the year after the accident, and Harriet the following year. They send Xmas cards and included photos of the children. No one could have a better monument to them, even the posthumous bravery award they gave me for him could never mean as much as those five beautiful children. Three of whom he saved from certain death.' Lauren was beaming with pride.

The women set to preparing the evening meal; they were eating early to give Val and Luke time to get home and to get the other children ready for bed.

They made a buffet style meal, filling the table with salads, pork pies, quiches, sausage rolls, as well as roast beef, pork, and chicken, with extra sausage for the kids. There was jelly, ice-cream, apple pie, and trifle for afters.

They then went outside for the fireworks. Zoe expected this as her birthday was on the third of November.

The men had lit a bonfire at the very end of the garden, which was bordered with fields so it was safe. The fireworks had lots of oohs and aahs coming from everyone there. They loved playing with the sparklers and the older kids made sure they were put in a bucket of water when finished. The rainbow colours of the Roman candles, the red, gold, and green from the traffic lights, the spinning stars from the Catherine wheels, and the whoosh and sprays of stars from the rockets all added to the thrill of the night.

It was a wonderful party and family gathering. In the glow of the fire, the happy smiling faces of the children, despite being covered in toffee from the toffee apples, and moustaches from the hot chocolate, made it all worthwhile.

Once the little ones were in bed, and Gail and Tony had gone to the sports centre with some friends, Les had taken Val and Luke to the station for their train. They all collapsed in chairs or on bean bags with a nice cold glass of wine.

'Oh boy, I'm knackered,' said Pete and echoed by the others, 'I won't be long before I'm in bed. I need a good night's sleep.'

'Well, you'd better go very soon, Pete.' Laughed Babs as the little ones will all be up before seven in morning.

Pat was very clever at following the conversation as long as she could see their mouths. She was an excellent lip-reader, and she was nodding and laughing with everyone else.

This happiness was well deserved by them all.

Chapter Fifty-seven

For the next few years, life continued to be happy, and in the most part, very contented. A few things had been very stressful, like Luke dying in his sleep in 1985. This was very distressing for everyone, but knowing it was going to happen had helped a little. Val was devastated at his death, until Babs and Pat had suggested she look after their foster children so Pat could work more hours. Val did help and was marvellous with the three children, who actually lived with the twins on a permanent basis. It had helped that they had taken the three of them, whereas people looking to adopt prefer babies and not three together.

Then the big surprise had been in 1987 when Babs announced she was getting married to a surgeon, Charles Wright, who she had been seeing for only four months. Jo knew how quickly she had fallen in love with Les, so she understood, they had flown out to Barbados to get married. Pat went with them while Val looked after the children.

When they returned, Babs, Charles, Pat, and the children moved into a six-bedroom house in Patrington, just outside Hull, which also had a granny flat at the back so Val could stay whenever she wanted, which Babs was pleased about the following year when she gave birth to twins Emily and Amy. There was a happy busy home with five children; however, Dawn was a great help and loved being the big 'sister' figure.

Amy was born deaf, but this was never a problem as everyone signed for Pat and Amy grew up learning.

Lauren had also married again in 1986, and everyone was delighted for her. Patrick Rogers was part of their ever-increasing family. Zoe loved him and her brothers—Adam who arrived in 1987 and Adrian who was born in 1989. Jo was convinced Harry was up there smiling down on them, and he would have been delighted that Lauren and Zoe were happy and cared for.

Malcolm and Annette also increased their family by having twins, Gemma and Maria, in 1984 and Sally-Anne in 1987.

The whole family were shocked at the number of twins around, who said they missed a generation.

Jo did have sad times when she wished she could have had Les's child. She loved her own more than anything, but because of how much she loved Les she would have loved his child.

The consultant had told them following her hysterectomy that the damage to her uterus probably was from when Tony was born had caused adhesions, and she could never have carried a baby full-term. Somehow, this helped her, although she held Roy responsible. He had thrown her downstairs and caused her to go into labour with Tony, and now she knew that was the damage he caused. This meant she had killed three children inside her and almost four. However, she was now so content, and the children were growing up into wonderful people so she was very happy.

Her nursing career had gone from strength to strength, and she loved it and was very proud of herself. She had enrolled at Leeds University where she gained a BA in nursing studies, commuted to the Royal Marsden in London to gain her oncology qualification, as she was working at Cookridge Hospital, which was the regional radiotherapy centre for Yorkshire and Lincolnshire, and in 1989, she achieved a teaching qualification to help her train nurses. Les had set up his own business leasing garage space, tools, and used his knowledge to help people repair their own cars. He eventually had four garages in West Yorkshire, and employed fifteen people, including eight mechanics to help the customers, and had a very good business.

They were both very proud when they attended Oxford University in 1987 for Gail's graduation. She had achieved a BA honours in modern languages and then stayed on to get an MA in modern languages and linguistics, which was the ceremony they were attending this time. Gail had also been offered a position as an interpreter at the Crown Court in Leeds, and she had accepted and they had even agreed to her having a three-month break before starting work. Gail was a home bird and had spent enough time away at Oxford so she was ready to come home. Les has hired a van to bring all of her things back with them. He had bought her a Nissan Micra as a graduation present, and Tony would travel home with Gail in her car. Les had taught them both to drive, and they passed their tests when they were seventeen.

Jo was positively bursting with pride as they announced 'Gail Williams, master of arts in modern languages and linguistics.' Gail stepped up to the rostrum in all her regalia. She was fluent in French, German, Spanish, Italian, and Russian and had enrolled part-time at Leeds University for Japanese and Chinese, which she could speak quite well because she had roomed with a girl from Japan and one from China, and they had been teaching her. 'Who would have thought they could have done all this,' Les leant over and whispered in her ear.

'Now you know how I felt at your graduation. I was so proud of you, just as I am of our Gail.'

They looked at Tony, who was applauding so loud, he loved his sister very much.

'It will be your turn soon, won't it, Tony?' Les said.

'Yes, Mr Tony Woodhouse, MD. Sounds good, but wait until it is Tony Woodhouse FRCS and who knows from there. I want to eventually work in cancer like Mum.'

When the four of them went out for a meal that night, they were beyond happiness. Jo could never have imagined life would be this good. Ben was married to Sheila and had also done very well with a degree in business studies and was running two businesses in double glazing. Roy was now an old man and not a problem to anyone, Jane was happy with her children and grandchildren, so Roy was the only one who had nothing. Jo had thought about what Nanna used to say, 'God doesn't pay his debts with money.' Very true!

The families Secrets and Lies were over, and would never arise again.

The End